Apple Watch Series 4

Telling Time & So Much More

Cathy Young
Michael Young

Apple Watch Series 4

Telling Time & So Much More

Copyright © 2018 by Cathy Young

Trademarks

Warning and Disclaimer

First Edition: December 2018

Table of Contents

Look Inside

- **The Apple Watch Series 4 uses the ECG app to record an electrocardiogram.** iOS 12.1.1 added blood pressure monitoring and irregular rhythm notifications. Instructions for using these apps and settings are outlined in Chapter 9.

- **If you have a hard fall, your Apple Watch will call for help.** See Chapter 2, Guide to Basics.

- **Set up a shared grocery list and add items with your digital assistant.** Everyone in your family can tap their wrist (or iPhone) to view and check off items on your family's grocery list. Use Siri, Alexa, Google Home, or Microsoft Cortana to add items to your grocery list. Chapter 7 covers setting up iOS family sharing and a shared iOS reminder list. Steps for creating IFTTT integrations that link iOS reminders and digital assistants are also included.

- **Learn how to set up custom app notifications.** Chapter 3 demonstrates calendar alerts, mail VIP alerts, Map driving alerts, Workout reminders and more.

- **Any app could include Apple Watch "Complications" for your watch face.** The LoseIt! app tracks daily calories, Pedometer shows steps today, and Audible reads your book. We'll show you how to add these complications to your customized watch faces in Chapter 4 and dig into all the details of complications.

- **Explore over 100 third-party apps in Chapter 7, including IFTTT.** When a manufacturer doesn't have an Apple Watch app, chances are they do have IFTTT integrations. Logitech Harmony, eBay, and Twitter IFTTT widgets are discussed in Chapter 7.

We also cover creating your own IFTTT applets and multi-step IFTTT Maker apps.

- **The Mickey or Minnie Mouse watch face will announce the time.** See Getting Started, "Sounds and Haptics" in Chapter 2. Personalize this watch face with "Magic Guide to Disney World." Chapter 4 Watch Faces has all the details on watch faces, and samples with suggested apps and configurations to try out.

- **Use Apple Pay & Apple Wallet on your watch.** Send money with Siri messages, pay a cashier, or tap your watch to approve that transaction you're completing in Safari on your Mac. Chapter 6 also explains the PassKit framework and how to add all types of cards, tickets, and passes to your Wallet app.

- **Unlock your Mac whenever your Apple Watch is in range.** Chapter 8, Day to Day has the details on "Continuity" features like Handoff and Auto Unlock.

- **In Chapter 7 learn how to control iTunes or an Apple TV with your Apple Watch.**

- **Use your Apple Watch as a camera remote control** to take photos with your iPhone. Chapter 5, Watch Apps, has the info.

- **Learn how to check your fitness progress** utilizing your Heart Rate Recovery data as discussed in Chapter 9.

- **The science of Haptics uses wrist vibrations to deliver alerts or notifications.** Apple Taptic Engine examples utilizing haptics include Map apps that gently vibrate the Apple Watch on your wrist to indicate an upcoming turn. Check out details in Chapter 10, Accessibility.

Preface

So, you have a new Apple Watch. A hearty congratulations to you! No doubt you've heard about messaging, email, and the health apps. The visionary Apple Watch is, at last, poised to take on the world in the Apple Watch Series 4! I want you to feel comfortable with all aspects of your watch in an environment that encourages you to learn painlessly at your own pace. My goal is to help you enjoy the wonder of discovering your Apple Watch. Along the way, I want to:

- Teach you how to use all the features of your Apple Watch. I say "all." As far as I know, I found every darned one of them but don't sue me if I missed one.

- Demonstrate the cool and awe-inspiring features of the Apple Watch. These aren't random tips and tricks. Rather, I have showcased them in a way that lets you find them while exploring a particular feature or topic.

- Help you find what you want, when you want it. The organized and detailed Table of Contents includes more than 200 topics. Skip around to your heart's content.

- Inspire you with over 100 third-party apps. A few of the categories include entertainment, productivity, sports, photography, and games. We'll also cover integration platforms like IFTTT, which open up the possibility of unlimited applications.

- Focus on the engineering and Apple platforms behind the Apple Watch. The physical device includes the heart rate monitor, accelerometer, gyroscope and Apple's Force Touch technology. Behind the scenes, learn how Apple is partnering with businesses to extend their HealthKit, HomeKit, and GymKit platforms to enhance your experience for years to come.

- List 30 Common Troubleshooting and Maintenance Suggestions.

This book is specifically for the Series 4 Apple Watch. While much of the content applies equally to older models, please know that I didn't attempt to cover discontinued features like "glances" or "time travel."

As a final selling point, I make an intentional effort to avoid a few of my pet peeves – and those pertain to incomplete (or half-a**ed) instructions. I frequently see directions such as "tap to go to settings," but they leave novice users asking, "tap where?" In another example I read, the instructions mentioned a workout playlist and how to enable it – but assumed nothing went awry (and something ALWAYS goes awry). I intend to cover those bases for you. And if I do, by chance, make the mistake of omitting a critical detail anywhere in this book, know that I was probably distracted by my Apple Watch telling me to get moving or to breathe. I apologize ahead of time; it wasn't intentional.

Are you ready for the Apple Watch experience? Let's get started.

6

1. Introduction

In this chapter we discuss

What is the Apple Watch?
Apple Watch Series 4
watchOS 5
What's Next?

Apple provided an interesting backstory when they unveiled the first Apple Watch. For those who recall the two-way wristwatch sported by Dick Tracy in the 1946 comic strip, this story will sound familiar. The animator, Chester Gould, visited the workshop of inventor Al Gross, who had a two-way radio wristwatch. Gould asked Gross for permission to use the idea in his comic strip; and, thus, inspired the Apple Watch.

Chapter 1

Gross was a true visionary. His patents for a garage door opener, cordless phone, and cell phone expired long before they became household objects. His ideas, however, for a beeper and Citizens Band (CB) radio system became hugely popular. His ground-to-air radio revolutionized communication during World War II.

When Apple first released their watch, I couldn't wait to try one. Although well engineered, the first Apple Watch wasn't quite what I was expecting. There wasn't a lot of support from third-party apps, no cellular service; and considering the steep price tag, I decided to try again on a future version.

A few years went by and I bought another watch that had a cellular option so I could listen to music on the go. This time I had the opposite problem. This Apple Watch had too many features and apps. Although all the answers were available on the Internet, I had neither the time nor patience to research them. Frankly, what I wanted was a personal help desk that I could call at a moment's notice. I think my solution to the problem was inspired. I gave the watch to my daughter with the understanding she would teach me how to use it in the future. (Want to guess how that idea played out?)

Fast forward to the arrival of the Apple Watch Series 4. I admit my daughter did help me through what I consider the hand-holding period - that first week or two where I wanted to receive calls and messages, listen to music, and set up a cool watch face. There was some teasing involved, but we both enjoyed the process. I took copious notes for future reference. I confess to having a bad memory, so I compensate by organizing and cross-referencing notes like a crazy person. Those notes, lovingly edited by my husband, evolved into the book that I hope you are about to read and deem worthy of the cost of a latte at Starbucks.

1.1 What is the Apple Watch?

At its simplest level, the Apple Watch is a digital timepiece with features and applications similar to a smartphone. When combined with an Apple iPhone, your Apple Watch Series 4 is an extraordinary tool, adapted to your preferences and lifestyle. Apple apps are free, and third-party apps are available for download from the Apple Store for a nominal amount – if not also free.

The Apple Watch is designed in part to improve your health. Forget workout or fitness apps for a moment. Fall detection, emergency SOS, and heart rate monitoring (including a new ECG app) are part of the health lineup. The "Breathe" or "Forest-Stay Focused" apps promote mindfulness. Recent research into the neuroscience of mindfulness shows deep breathing reduces stress and has long-term health benefits. The workout and fitness apps are impressive. Your health goals, moreover, get a huge boost from these Apple Watch features.

Receive messages, stream music, and use Apple Pay or Siri with your Apple Watch. These features are not dependent on your iPhone when you purchase Apple Watch models that include built-in cellular. Keep in mind, however, that an airtime contract with your cellular carrier is required for cellular models.

The Apple Watch supports several faces that you can customize to your heart's content. Pick the apps you want on your watch and then decide how to arrange them. In Chapter 4, we discuss app "complications" for your watch face. A complication example is a small icon or text that represents an app like your calendar or calorie counter.

Apple has unique and defined iOS terminology in their "Human Interface Guidelines." These guidelines are not just terms for the interface icons, tab bars, sliders and switches. We humans come into play here because we're the ones swiping, tapping, and probably cursing a bit as we learn the Force Touch Technology (FTT). Touch gestures are used to navigate to these areas and I have outlined them in the next chapter.

1.2 Apple Watch Series 4

Apple says the Apple Watch Series 4 represents a fundamental redesign and re-engineering of Apple Watch. The watch ships with the watchOS 5 mobile operating system which encompasses the logistics of how the Apple Watch works. The 16GB storage capacity is ideal for podcasts, music and photo storage. The new S4 64 bit dual-core processor is up to two times faster than the Series 3. The watch uses Bluetooth 5, which has more speed, better range, and lower power consumption.

The Apple Watch Series 4 LTPO OLED retina display is 30% larger than previous models. Apple's patent "Liquid Crystal Displays with Oxide-Based Thin-Film Transistors" includes technology designed to extend battery life. The Digital Crown now provides haptic feedback with the sensation of incremental clicks.

The built-in rechargeable lithium-ion battery uses magnetic charging and lasts up to 18 hours. The power saving Bluetooth 5 and LTPO display are two of the reasons for the longer battery life.

Chapter 1

The microphone is now on the other side of the watch, away from the speaker. The microphone location reduces echo for better sound quality. Audio volume is also 50% louder to accommodate the new walkie-talkie app.

Features like a heart rate monitor, improved accelerometer, barometric altimeter, and gyroscope are ideal for health and fitness apps. The accelerometer can differentiate between a walk and a run and enables features like "Running Auto Pause" to identify when you're taking an exercise break.

The black ceramic back has a sapphire crystal and electrical heart rate sensors. Radio waves easily pass through the front and back for better cellular service. The case comes in aluminum or stainless steel.

- Stainless steel is heavier and has a shiny appearance, while the aluminum has a matte finish.

- The crystal sapphire glass on the stainless steel model resists scratches better than the Ion-X glass on the aluminum model.

The new Apple ECG app arrived with watchOS 5.1.2 and iOS 12.1.1. The ECG app provides heart rate monitoring similar to an electrocardiogram (EKG). The app was granted the De Novo classification by the FDA in the U.S. for the ECG and atrial fibrillation detection features. The ECG app works by measuring your heart rate on your wrist while you touch the opposite hand to the electrode in the Digital Crown, creating a circuit.

If the Apple Watch detects a significant, hard fall while you're wearing your watch, it taps you on the wrist, sounds an alarm, and displays an alert. If you do not respond to the prompt, your watch will automatically contact emergency services.

1.3 watchOS 5

The watchOS 5 operating system encompasses the logistics of how the Apple Watch works. The watchOS supports your interaction with your Apple Watch - tapping, swiping and controls. This engineering is elegant and simple to use, and provides Wi-Fi and Bluetooth connectivity, pairing to your companion iPhone, and app updates from the Apple Store. These are some interesting new features in watchOS 5.

- Activity Competitions
- Challenge a friend

- Personalized coaching, awards, cadence

- Seven-day competition - Win the week!

- Student ID Cards

- Walkie-Talkie

- Podcasts

- Raise to speak (to Siri)

- Two new wheelchair workouts take into account different pushing conditions. Wheelchair mode in the Health app enables "Roll Goals" and "Time to Roll" notifications, and the Activity app counts pushes instead of steps.

- Schedule Do Not Disturb for a specific time or until you leave your location.

1.4 What's Next?

At this point are you thinking this all sounds a bit complicated? There's new jargon to learn (haptics, complications, watch faces, apps), and it can be both intimidating and frustrating. Don't despair - we'll take this one step at a time.

So now, are you wearing your Apple Watch with your iPhone nearby? You're ready to tackle this amazing gadget, so let us move on to Chapter 2.

Chapter 1

2. Setup & Getting Started

In this chapter we discuss

Force Touch

Human Interface Guidelines

A Quick Look at Watch Controls

Turn On or Wake

Charging the Watch

Turn Off

Pair Your Watch & iPhone

Rename Your Watch

Setup Cellular Service

Passcode & Security Features

The Display

Chapter 2

The Home Screen

The Side Button & Dock

Digital Crown

Control Center

Heart Sensors & Electrodes

Band Release Buttons

Brightness & Text

Sounds & Haptics

Change the Time Shown

Apple Resources

What's Next?

Chapter 2 is meant to get you started quickly with your new Apple Watch. This chapter is laid out as a handy reference, so it should be easy to return and find what you're looking for at any time. You'll learn how to:

- Pair your watch with your iPhone.

- Setup cellular service.

- Complete basic setup steps.

- Manipulate basic controls.

Settings are configured on your Apple Watch or in the Apple Watch app on your iPhone. On your watch, open the "Settings" app or swipe up to open "Control Center." On your iPhone, open the Apple Watch App and swipe to see various options.

- General
- Brightness & Text Size
- Sounds & Haptics
- Passcode
- Emergency SOS
- Privacy
- Change the Time Shown

2.1 Force Touch

Touch gestures may be a new world for some. I wanted to briefly cover these terms before jumping into details. As a functioning adult, I have a pretty good handle on clicking buttons and turning knobs. I have even adapted to tapping or swiping on my smartphone, tablet screen, or Mac trackpad.

Apple introduced Force Touch Technology (FTT) in 2014 with its first Apple Watch. It is available today on several Apple products, including touch pads and the iPhone. The screen display, digital crown, and side button support FTT. The screen of the Apple Watch responds to taps, swipes, or firm presses. In the case of the side button on the Apple Watch, it responds differently to a gentle press compared to when you press down and hold it.

- Swipe - Touch the screen with one finger and slide your finger in the direction indicated without lifting your finger: left, right, up or down.

- Tap - Quickly touch the screen with a light touch and release.

- Firm Press - Press down on the screen with a firm touch.

- Drag- Touch a selection on the screen with your finger and slide your finger across the screen without lifting.

2.2 Human Interface Guidelines

Apple developers, no doubt, are cringing when they read instructions that use the wrong terminology for those switches, sliders and tab bars. I made a serious effort to use the right terms: toggle the switch, move the slider. But I will say I absolutely could not find the appropriate name for the icon that looks like three horizontal bars that you grab to move songs in a playlist or reorder apps. Please, if you know the term for that stupid icon, post a review comment!

- Switch - toggle a feature on or off. Green is on, white is off.

- Sliders - touch the slider bar and move the bar.

- Three horizontal bars - touch, hold and drag to rearrange items in a list.

- Add - this icon looks like a plus **+** symbol.

- More - this icon looks like an ellipsis or three dots.

- Mark Location - this icon looks like a pin on a map.

- Tab bar - icons in a row along the bottom of the screen.

2.3 A Quick Look at Watch Controls

Three physical characteristics of your Apple Watch to which we will refer again and again are the Display, the Digital Crown and the Side Button.

Figure 2.1   The Watch Face Controls

A - Display

B - Digital Crown

C - Microphone

D - Side Button

2.4 Turn On or Wake

There are several ways to turn on, or wake, your Apple Watch. These options are configurable as outlined in the Chapter 3 topic "Wake Screen on Wrist Raise" listed under "General Settings."

- Lift your wrist or tap the screen to wake your watch.

- Gradually turn the Digital Crown on your Apple Watch to slowly brighten the screen and discreetly check the time.

- On the Apple Watch, press and hold the side button.

2.5 Charging the Watch

The charging cable attaches to the back of your watch as shown in Figure 2.2. A green lightning bolt symbol appears on the watch face when your Apple Watch is connected to a charging cable. The lightning bolt symbol is red when your watch needs charging. It may take a few minutes for the green lightning bolt symbol to appear if your battery level is low.

Chapter 2

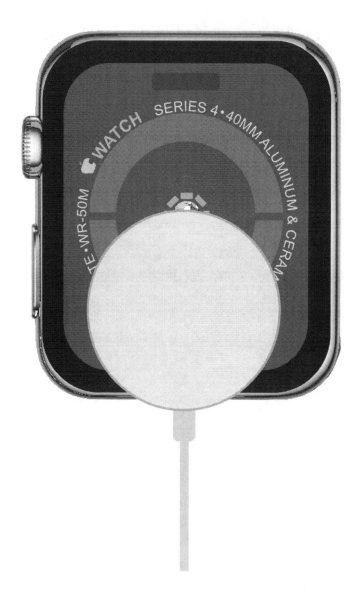

Figure 2.2   The Charging Cable

To troubleshoot charging try these suggestions.

1.   Completely remove any plastic wrap from both sides of the charger.

2.   Plug the charger into a different cable or power outlet.

3.   Reset your watch.

2.6 Turn Off

Place your palm over the watch face for a few seconds to turn off the screen. The "Cover to Mute" option is configurable along with Silent or Theater Mode as shown in Settings, Sounds & Haptics. Follow these steps to turn off your watch.

1.   On the Apple Watch, press and hold the side button until the menu appears.

2.   Touch the "Power Off" slider and drag to the right to turn off your watch.

3.   Press and hold the side button to turn your watch back on.

25

2.7 Pair Your Watch & iPhone

Pairing your Apple Watch with a companion iPhone unlocks the full potential of the Apple Watch. I recommend that you have a fully charged battery before starting the pairing process.

1. Turn on the Apple Watch and the iPhone.

2. Hold your Apple Watch near your iPhone and wait for the message, "Use this iPhone to set up your Apple Watch." If you don't see the message, open the Apple Watch app on your iPhone and tap "start pairing."

3. Follow the prompts and wait for the devices to sync. The synchronization can take a while so this might be a good time to get a cup of coffee or do your taxes. Don't be impatient, as I was, or you will interrupt the process and have to start over.

In case you replace or upgrade your iPhone, you needn't be concerned about your Health and Activity data. iCloud with the iPhone iOS version 11 stores "Health and Activity data" automatically. The only requirement is that you are signed in with the same Apple ID on all devices.

2.8 Rename Your Watch

To rename your watch, open the Apple Watch app on your iPhone.

1.   On the iPhone, open the Apple Watch app.

2.   Tap "My Watch," located in the left corner of the tab bar at the bottom of the screen.

3.   Scroll down to "General."

4.   Under "About," tap "Name."

2.9 Setup Cellular Service

You can activate a cellular network when you first set up your Apple Watch. During setup, look for the option to set up cellular, then follow the on-screen steps.

Although your Apple Watch will have a separate phone number from your carrier once you sign up for an airtime contract, your watch will use your companion iPhone number as well.

You can also set up cellular later from the Apple Watch app:

1. On the iPhone, open the Apple Watch app.

2. Tap the My Watch tab, then tap "Cellular."

3. Tap "Set Up Cellular."

4. Follow the instructions for your carrier. You might need to contact your carrier for help.

There are two separate models for Apple Watch Series 4, optimized for the country of purchase to support LTE and UMTS bands used around the world.

To check cellular data usage on your iPhone, open the Apple Watch app. Usage is shown for the current period, as well as for each app.

1. On the iPhone, open the Apple Watch app.

2. Tap the My Watch tab, then tap "Cellular."

3. Swipe to see cellular data usage for apps.

2.10 Passcode & Security Features

A 4-digit passcode secures your watch from unauthorized use. Although you can choose to turn passcode off, that option removes Apple Pay from your Apple Watch. You can enter the passcode with these passcode settings.

- Simple Passcode (4-Digit)
- Unlock with iPhone

If you want a passcode longer than four digits turn off simple passcode. The "Erase Data" option will protect your watch in case your watch is lost or stolen. It erases all data after ten failed attempts.

Change Passcode Options

1. Open the Apple Watch app on your iPhone.

2. Tap "My Watch," located in the left corner of the tab bar at the bottom of the screen.

3. Scroll down to "Passcode."

4. Touch the "Unlock with iPhone" switch to toggle on or off.

Wrist Detection

Wrist Detection is a security measure to lock your watch when you're not wearing it. Follow these steps to turn on Wrist Detection.

1. Open the Apple Watch app on your iPhone.

2. Tap "My Watch," located in the left corner of the tab bar at the bottom of the screen.

3 Tap "Passcode."

4. Swipe up, then tap "Wrist Detection." A green slider bar indicates Wrist Detection is on.

Clear Website Data

Another security feature new to the Apple Watch Series 4 is the ability to delete browsing data from your watch.

1. On the Apple Watch press the side button.

2. Swipe and tap on "Settings."

3.   Tap "General" and scroll to "Website Data."

4.   Tap "Clear Website Data."

Turn on Find My Watch

By default, "Find My Watch" is turned on after pairing your watch to your companion iPhone.

1.   On the iPhone open "Settings."

2.   Tap "your name," and then scroll down and tap your Series 4 Apple Watch.

3.   Ensure "Find My Watch" is turned on.

Find Your Apple Watch

In case you lose your watch, you can use the "Find My iPhone" app to locate it. If you have an Apple HomePod your can say, "Hey Siri, find my watch." The app also has options to turn on "Lost Mode." Lost mode locks your watch and displays a custom message.

1. On the iPhone open the "Find My iPhone" app and sign in.

2. Tap your Apple Watch to locate your watch on a map.

3. Tap "Actions" to play a sound, erase the watch, or turn on lost mode.

2.11 The Display

When you wake your watch the watch face is displayed. Status icons in the middle along the top edge of the watch face indicate when you have a notification, or an alert that your battery needs charging. Status icons are discussed in detail in Chapter 3. The Notification Center is covered in Chapter 5.

Press the watch face display firmly to change the watch face or see options in an app.

2.12 The Home Screen

The Home screen is a list of apps installed on your watch, shown in grid or list view. Press the Digital Crown to see the Home screen.

Home - Grid or List View

The Home screen has a grid or list view. The grid view resembles a honeycomb. I found getting comfortable to this view difficult and decided to switch from "Grid View" to "List View." Of course, then it drove me crazy that I couldn't remember how to go back to the honeycomb style grid view. Now I mostly hang out in List View, but at least I know how to change between the two.

To move around the Home Screen grid view, turn the Digital Crown to zoom in or zoom out. Continue zooming in to see a preview of the app, and keep turning the Digital Crown to open the app. To reposition the app icons, touch the screen and hold, and slide your finger on the screen to reposition the focus.

Switch Between Grid or List View

With the Home screen open, firmly press the screen and then tap either "Grid" or "List View."

Reset Home Screen Layout to Factory Default

1. On the iPhone, open the Apple Watch app.

2. Tap "My Watch," located in the left corner of the tab bar at the bottom of the screen.

3. Tap "General" and then tap "Reset Home Screen Layout".

2.13 Side Button & Dock

Press the Side Button to show the Dock. Double-click the Side Button to open Apple Pay. Press and hold the Side Button to turn your Apple Watch on or off or to call emergency services.

Figure 2.3   The Side Button

The Dock is a list of up to ten of your favorite apps. I change my Dock frequently, swapping apps in and out as needed. To see all apps available to the dock, tap the side button on your watch.

1. On the Apple Watch, press the "Side Button."

2. Swipe up to the end of the list and tap "All Apps."

Follow these steps to configure which apps appear in the Dock.

1. On the iPhone, open the Apple Watch app.

2. Tap "My Watch," located at the left corner of the tab bar at the bottom of the screen.

3. Tap the "Dock."

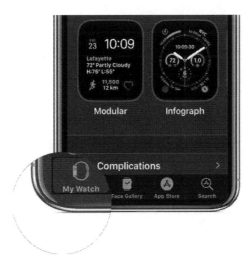

Figure 2.4   The Apple Watch App

4. In the section "Dock Ordering," tap
    "Favorites" to choose which apps appear
    in the Dock.

5. Scroll to find apps and tap more (the plus
    symbol) to add the app to favorites.

Add an App to The Dock

1. On the Apple Watch, press the side button
    and tap on the app.

2. Swipe and tap on "Add to Dock." This
    option is not available if you already have
    ten favorite apps.

Reorder the List of Apps

1. On the iPhone, open the Apple Watch app.

2. Tap "My Watch," located in the left corner of the tab bar at the bottom of the screen.

3. Tap "Dock."

4. Tap "Edit."

On the right side of the app name, tap the three lines and drag the app name to a different location in the list.

Remove an App from the Dock

To conserve battery power, remove apps you don't use from the Dock. To check battery levels, swipe up on the Apple Watch face to open Control Center, then swipe to see battery life.

- On the Apple Watch, open The Dock and tap an app.

- When the app is open, swipe left and tap the red X.

2.14 The Digital Crown

When I was learning to use my Apple Watch, I had no idea the Digital Crown was the gateway to hundreds of options. Although you can press it to wake your watch and go to your Home screen, that is just the tip of the iceberg. Press the Digital Crown to see the Home screen. Press and hold the Digital Crown to start Siri. Turn the Digital Crown to scroll or zoom.

Turn the Digital Crown wheel to scroll through complications, lists, settings, and a myriad of other features - the Digital Crown zooms in and out of maps. Turning the Digital Crown creates a time-lapse effect as the sun moves across the Earth watch face, or the planets align in the Solar System watch face as the days scroll by.

Explore the Digital Crown

The following is a list of interesting things you can do with the Digital Crown.

1. On the Apple Watch, press the Digital Crown in the center to access the Home screen.

2. Press and hold for Siri.

3. Turn the Digital Crown to move through the days of the week in the Calendar app.

We can see another fun demonstration of the Digital Crown in action with weather apps. Let's say you added a weather app complication to your watch face. Tap to select the weather complication and turn the Digital Crown to see the hourly forecast, air quality, UV index, wind index, and the 7-day forecast. Cool, huh? When displaying the "hourly forecast," tap the screen and it shows you the temperature; tap again, and it shows you rainfall.

The "Maps" app is another elegant example of the Digital Crown in action. On your Apple Watch, press the side button, swipe, and tap "Maps." Tap "Location," and then turn the Digital Crown to zoom in or out.

Switch Between Apps

To switch between the last two apps, double-click the Digital Crown.

Gradually Wake Your Watch

When your watch is asleep, gently turn the Digital Crown slowly to brighten the screen, and discreetly check the time.

2.15 Control Center

The Control Center has a series of icons. Swipe up on the Apple Watch face to open the Control Center. Tap to toggle the options on or off.

- Cellular
- Wi-Fi
- Airplane Mode
- Battery
- Find my iPhone
- Flashlight
- Do Not Disturb
- Mute
- Theater Mode
- Water Lock
- Audio Output

Tip: With watchOS 5 you can open Control Center from any screen. Touch the bottom of the screen until a semi-transparent preview of the Control Center appears, then swipe up.

Cellular

When connected the cellular status icon is green. When there is no connection, the status icon is grey.

Wi-Fi

When connected the Wi-Fi status icon is blue. When there is no connection, the status icon is grey.

Airplane Mode

An orange airplane means Airplane Mode is active.

Battery

The battery status icon displays your battery level as a percentage. A red icon indicates your battery is low.

Tip: The battery level of paired AirPods is also shown on the status screen.

Figure 2.5   Battery Level of Paired AirPods

Find My iPhone

Find My iPhone may be the handiest feature if you tend to misplace your iPhone as frequently as do I! Swipe up on your watch face and tap the icon to sound an alert on your companion iPhone instantly. The blue icon has an iPhone with signal bars. At night, touch and hold the icon to flash a light on your iPhone.

Flashlight

The flashlight setting has three modes: the basic light, a strobe light, or a red light. Swipe to the left or right to choose your setting. When running at night, the strobe light is a nice safety feature. Press the Digital Crown to turn off the flashlight, or tap the icon in Control Center.

Do Not Disturb

Calls and alerts won't ring or light up the screen when "Do Not Disturb" is on. Alarms will still sound. The Do Not Disturb status icon on your watch face is a blue moon. You can continue a "Walkie-Talkie" conversation if you turn on "Do Not Disturb," but other calls are silenced.

Silent Mode

Silent Mode will mute your watch. If you turn on Silent Mode while using the "Walkie-Talkie" app, you can still hear chimes and your friend's voice.

Chapter 2

Theater Mode

The picture of two masks is orange when Theater Mode is active. The screen stays dark and silent mode is also active until you tap the screen or press a button. When Theater Mode is active your Walkie-Talkie status is "unavailable."

Walkie-Talkie

The walkie-talkie icon is a stylized walkie-talkie radio. The icon appears after you create a connection with a contact. The icon is yellow when walkie-talkie is turned on, and indicates your status in the Walkie-Talkie app is "available."

Water Lock

As I type this, I'm looking over my shoulder expecting someone to say, "No way; you can't do that!" But this is straight from the horse's mouth (Apple being the horse) - you can go for a swim with your Apple Watch. Not only that, the Workout App has an option for "Open

Water Swim" or "Pool Swim." The "Water Lock" option is turned on automatically when you start one of these workouts and locks the screen to avoid accidental taps.

Turn on Water Lock

- On the Apple Watch, swipe up from the bottom of the screen to open Control Center.

- Tap the water lock icon. It looks like a drop of water.

Turn off Water Lock

When your workout ends, turn the Digital Crown to unlock the screen and clear water from the speaker. Turn the Digital Crown until you fill the "blue circle" on the screen. When complete, an alert sounds and the screen displays the message "Unlocked."

Audio Output

To stream music or videos to your favorite speakers, AirPods, or headsets, use the Audio Output in the Control Center.

1. Swipe up on the Apple Watch face to open Control Center.

2. Tap the Audio Output icon.

Tapping the audio output icon will also switch audio output between paired Bluetooth devices.

Control Audio Volume

Tap the audio status icon on your watch face, and turn the Digital Crown to adjust volume. Control music, podcasts, or hearing aid volume.

Rearrange Icons in the Control Center

To customize your Control Center apps, or set the app order, follow these steps.

1. Swipe up on the Apple Watch face to open the Control Center.

2. Swipe up and scroll to the end. Tap "Edit" to change items in the Control Center.

2.16 Heart Rate Sensors & Electrodes

The new ECG app provides heart rate monitoring similar to an electrocardiogram (EKG). The ECG app utilizes the electrical heart sensor, built-in electrodes, and the optical heart sensor.

2.17 Band Release Buttons

Changing watch bands seemed daunting to me at first, but after doing it one time I realized how simple it is.

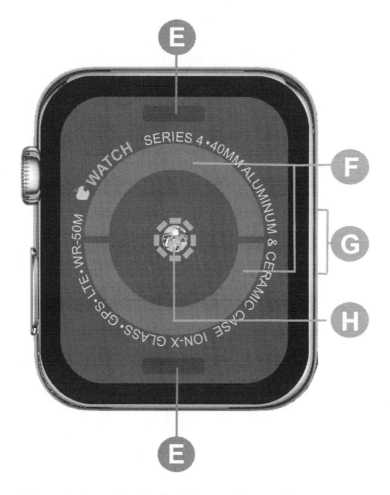

Figure 2.6   The Back of the Apple Watch

E - Band Release Buttons

F - Electrical heart sensor/built-in electrodes

G - Speaker/air vents

H - Optical Heart Sensor

1.   Place your watch face down on a soft
      surface.

2.   Press the band release button on the back
      on the watch and slide the band left or
      right to remove it from the slot.

3.   Slide the new band into the slot until you
      feel and hear a click.

      The end of the watch band that slides into
the slot has a top and bottom. The top has three
clips. The bottom has two clips on each end with
a solid piece in the middle. If you reverse the top
and bottom the band will not lock in place.

2.18 Brightness & Text

      Configure brightness, text size, and bold
text in the Apple Watch app on your iPhone.

1.   Open the Apple Watch app on your
      iPhone.

2.   Tap "My Watch," located in the left corner
      of the tab bar at the bottom of the screen.

3.   Scroll down to "Brightness & Text Size."

2.19 Sounds & Haptics

The standard sound options are available under "Sounds & Haptics." I found two options to be very creative. The "Cover to Mute" option will silence alerts and mute your watch when you place your palm over the watch face for at least three seconds. Disney fans will appreciate the "Tap to Speak" option that pairs with the Mickey or Minnie Mouse watch face.

- Alert Volume

- Silent Mode

- Haptic Alerts

- Cover to Mute

- Tap to Speak (Mickey or Minnie Mouse)

Haptics is the science of applying tactile sensation (touch) and control when interacting with computer applications. Apple introduced the Taptic Engine with the iPhone 6s. Chances are, you've found your muted iPhone at one time or another by following the vibrations. Haptics is also a useful accessibility feature for deaf or hard of hearing users, and drivers will appreciate the Map app that gently vibrates your Apple Watch to indicate an upcoming turn.

The options for haptic intensity are Default or Prominent. I haven't tried Prominent yet because I'm a little gun shy. There was an incident in which we purchased a dog collar deterrent. I said, "I'm not putting that on the dog unless I know what it feels like first." During the test, I seem to recall a knee-jerk reaction that involved throwing it across the room to get it as far away as possible from my body. I also recall several loud vocal outbursts. Okay, I may have cursed. Fortunately for our dog, the collar didn't work through his thick fur, so he never got to experience haptics first hand. But I did!

Since it's related to sound, let me mention that I cover how to pair Bluetooth speakers in the next section "Audio Output."

Adjust Volume

1. Open the Apple Watch app on your iPhone.

2. Tap "My Watch," located in the left corner of the tab bar at the bottom of the screen.

3. Scroll down and tap "Sounds & Haptics."

4. Touch the slider and drag it to adjust the Alert Volume.

Cover to Mute

The "Cover to Mute" setting means you can place your hand over the watch face to silence your Apple Watch and turn off the display.

Haptic Alerts

Haptics also play a role in alerts. For example, the Map app gently vibrates to indicate an upcoming turn. Haptic alerts are a useful accessibility feature for deaf or hard of hearing drivers.

1. On the iPhone open the Apple Watch app.

2. In the "Sounds & Haptics" section, tap the "Haptic Alerts" switch to toggle the switch on or off. The switch is green when on and white when off.

There is also an option to change the strength of the haptic alert to "Prominent."

Silent Mode

Silent mode is used to mute your Apple Watch. In comparison, "Do Not Disturb" keeps alerts and calls from lighting the screen. The options can be controlled on your Apple Watch in the Control Center or the Settings screen; or they can be set in the Apple Watch app on your iPhone. Silent mode will not silence alarms and timers when Apple Watch is charging.

Here we will look at three ways to control Silent Mode. There is also an option called "Cover to Mute" outlined earlier in the "Sounds & Haptics" discussion. When "Cover to Mute" is enabled, placing your hand over the screen for three seconds will silence your watch.

1. Open the Apple Watch app on your iPhone.

2. Tap "My Watch," located in the left corner of the tab bar at the bottom of the screen.

3. Scroll down to "Sounds & Haptics."

4. Tap the "Silent Mode" switch to toggle the switch on or off. The switch is green when on and white when off.

The sound icon (that looks like a bell) turns red to indicate silent mode is active. The sound icon turns green when sound is enabled. Silent Mode can also be controlled on your Apple Watch.

1. Press the side button on your Apple Watch to open "The Dock."

2. Scroll down and tap "Settings."

3. Scroll down and tap "Sounds & Haptics."

4. Tap the "Silent Mode" switch to toggle it on or off.

The Control Center has a Silent Mode toggle that also mutes your Apple Watch.

1. Swipe up on the Apple Watch face to open Control Center.

2. Tap the "Silent Mode" icon.

Do Not Disturb

Obviously, the Apple engineers put a lot of thought into the "Do Not Disturb" option. It is configurable for 1 hour, till this evening, or until you leave the current geofencing location.

1. Swipe up on the Apple Watch face to open Control Center.

2. Tap the "Do Not Disturb" switch (that looks like a moon). The switch is purple when on and grey when off. The Do Not Disturb status icon on your watch face is a blue moon.

When "Tap to Mirror iPhone" is also enabled, turning on "Do Not Disturb" on your Apple Watch also turns on "Do Not Disturb" on your iPhone, and vice versa.

1. Open the Apple Watch app on your iPhone.

2. Tap "My Watch," located in the left corner of the tab bar at the bottom of the screen.

3. Scroll down to "Sounds & Haptics."

4. Touch the "Do Not Disturb" switch to toggle it on or off. The switch is purple when on and grey when off.

2.20 Change the Time Shown

You can set the display time on the watch face ahead. The time does not change in any apps; the time displayed only changes on the watch face.

1. Press the side button on your Apple Watch to open the Dock.

2. Tap the gear icon to open "Settings." If you don't see the gear, touch the watch face and move your finger until you locate the gear icon.

3. Swipe and select "Time."

4. Tap the option "Set Watch Face Display Time Ahead."

2.21 Apple Resources

In addition to the online manual and copious articles, Apple goes above and beyond with these options to ensure you enjoy your Apple Watch.

- Apple Care

- A personal training session

- The Apple Support App

- The user guide "Apple Watch watchOS 5"

After two unfortunate incidents that involved water, now I always purchase Apple Care for my devices. I admit that I reacted in disbelief when my daughter explained how her phone slipped out of her back pocket into the water. However, the insurance representative said that is a common claim and he wasn't at all surprised.

Shortly after my watch arrived at my house, I received an email from Apple asking me if I would like a personal training session. I thought, "Why, thank you; I would." A personal training class seems like a thoughtful and personal touch on Apple's part. Last but not least, you can download the user manual "Apple Watch watchOS 5" in iBooks for free. That's the next best thing to buying this book!

2.22 What's Next?

The next chapter on basic features continues the setup process, explaining the options so you can select the features that interest you.

3. General Settings

In this chapter we discuss

Edit General Settings
Automatic App Install
Watch Orientation (Wrist)
Wake Screen
Nightstand Mode
Language and Region
Siri
Location Services
Accessibility
Handoff
Enable Screenshots
What's Next?

General settings on your watch control much of the functionality of your Apple Watch. The settings do vary slightly between your Apple Watch and the Apple Watch app on your iPhone. The numbered, step-by-step instructions that follow highlight how to update General Settings.

- About
- Orientation
- Automatic App Install
- Wake Screen
- Nightstand Mode
- Location Services
- Accessibility
- Website Data
- Siri
- Workout
- Regulatory
- Reset

3.1 Edit General Settings

1. On your Apple Watch, press the Digital Crown.

2. Tap "Settings" and then tap "General" to configure these settings.

3.2 Automatic App Install

When "Automatic App Install" is on, iPhone apps that work with your Apple Watch will automatically appear on your Apple Watch Home screen.

1. On your iPhone, open the Apple Watch App.

2. Tap "My Watch," located in the left corner of the tab bar along the bottom of the screen.

3. Scroll down to "General."

4. Tap the "Automatic App Install" switch to toggle on or off. The switch is green when on and white when off.

3.3 Watch Orientation (Wrist)

Open the Apple Watch app on your iPhone to set the orientation. This feature accommodates both left-handed or right-handed individuals. It is also handy for yoga workouts, to avoid bumping the Digital Crown.

1. On your iPhone, open the Apple Watch App.

2. Tap "My Watch," located in the left corner of the tab bar along the bottom of the screen.

3. Scroll down to "General."

4. Under "Watch Orientation," select left or right wrist.

If your Apple watch doesn't wake when you raise your wrist, check the orientation of the digital crown and the "wake screen on wrist raise" settings.

3.4 Wake Screen

The "Wake Screen" options configure four settings as shown below.

1. Wake Screen on Wrist Raise.
2. Wake Screen on Crown Up.
3. Auto-launch Audio Apps.
4. On-Screen Wake Show Last App.

Gradually Wake Your Watch

When your watch is asleep, gently turn the Digital Crown to brighten the screen slowly and discreetly check the time.

Lift Your Wrist to Wake Your Watch

When "Wake Screen on Wrist Raise" is enabled, lift your wrist to wake your watch. This feature can be distracting if you sleep with your watch on so, on those occasions where I'm monitoring my sleep, I turn off "Wake Screen on Wrist Raise."

1. On your Apple Watch, press the Side Button.

2. Tap "Settings," and then tap "General."

3. Scroll down and tap "Wake."

4. Scroll down to the section "Wake Screen on Wrist Raise."

If your Apple watch doesn't wake when you raise your wrist, check the orientation of the Digital Crown and the "Wake Screen on Wrist Raise" settings.

1. Open the Apple Watch app on your iPhone.

2. Tap "My Watch," located in the left corner of the tab bar along the bottom of the screen.

3. Scroll down to "General."

4. Under "Watch Orientation" select left or right wrist.

Return to Last Activity on Screen Raise

When you wake your watch, it opens to the Home screen of the digital clock. On the General -> "Settings" screen, you can configure your Apple Watch to return to your last activity when you raise your wrist.

1. On your Apple Watch, press the Digital Crown.

2. Tap "Settings," and then tap "General."

3. Scroll down and tap "Wake."

4. Scroll down to the section "On-Screen Raise Show Last App" and tap your selection.

3.5 Nightstand Mode

Use your Apple Watch as a nightstand clock while charging. If there is an alarm set, the screen will gently brighten before the alarm.

1. On your iPhone, open the Apple Watch app.

2. Swipe to scroll down to "Settings" and tap "General."

3. Touch the "Nightstand Mode" slider and continue holding the slider as you move it to enabled. The slider is green when enabled and white when disabled.

Set an Alarm

1. On your Apple Watch, press the side button to open The Dock.

2. Swipe to scroll and tap the "Alarms" app.

3. Tap "Add alarm."

4. Turn the Digital Crown to adjust the alarm time.

5. Tap "Set."

6. Tap the new alarm to set options for repeat, or to change the alarm name.

3.6 Language and Region

Change the language or region in the Apple Watch app on your iPhone in the "General" settings. The region must be China for Apple Pay transit cards.

3.7 Siri

If you don't use "Hey Siri" turn it off to save battery power.

1. On your Apple Watch, press the Side Button.

2. Tap "Settings," and then tap General.

3. Scroll down and tap "Siri."

4. Tap the "Hey Siri" switch to toggle on or off. The switch is green when on and white when off.

3.8 Location Services

Enable location services for a more accurate reading of the distances you travel.

1. On your iPhone, go to Settings, Privacy, Location Services, and make sure Location Services is turned on.

2. Near the top of the list of apps, select Apple Watch Faces and Apple Watch Workout and select the option "While Using the App."

3.9 Accessibility

Now that I am of a certain age, accessibility features take on a whole new meaning. Since I love large text and LED flashing alerts on my iPhone, I thought I'd check out what settings are available on the Apple Watch. These accessibility settings are also discussed in Chapter 10, along with Vision, Hearing, and Physical & Motor Skills features unique to the Apple Watch.

- VoiceOver
- Zoom
- Grayscale
- Bold Text
- Reduce Motion
- Reduce Transparency
- On/Off Labels
- Side Button Click Speed

The apps are designed with accessibility in mind. Two new wheelchair workouts take into account different pushing conditions. Wheelchair mode in the Health app enables "Roll Goals" and "Time to Roll" notifications. The Activity app counts "pushes" instead of steps. The new Walkie-Talkie app instantly starts a conversation at a touch of your finger. Haptics (wrist taps) also play a role in alerts. For example, the Map app gently vibrates to indicate an upcoming turn. Haptics is a useful accessibility feature for deaf or hard of hearing drivers. There are several ways to enable accessibility features.

- On your Apple Watch, go to Settings.

- Triple-click the Digital Crown.

- On your iPhone, in the Apple Watch app go to the Accessibility screen.

Accessibility Shortcut

The "Accessibility Shortcut" uses the Digital Crown to turn on "Zoom" or "VoiceOver" with a triple-click.

1. Open the Apple Watch app on your iPhone.

2. Tap My Watch, go to "General."

3. Tap Accessibility, then tap "Accessibility Shortcut."

4. Choose "VoiceOver" or "Zoom."

Chapter 3

VoiceOver

Siri excels at toggling VoiceOver on or off. Press the Digital Crown to wake up Siri and say, "Turn on VoiceOver." Siri responds with "VoiceOver on." If you prefer, you can turn on VoiceOver in "Settings."

1. On your Apple Watch, press the Side Button.

2. Tap "Settings," and then tap General.

3. Swipe to select Accessibility.

4. Tap "VoiceOver" to toggle on or off.

Zoom

The "Zoom" feature will magnify the Apple Watch display. Press the Digital Crown to wake up Siri and say, "Turn on Zoom." There is a setting for the Digital Crown to turn either VoiceOver or Zoom on with a triple-click.

1. On your iPhone, open the Apple Watch app.

2. Tap My Watch, go to "General."

3. Tap "Accessibility," then tap the "Zoom" switch to toggle it on or off and set the zoom level.

3.10 Handoff

Handoff is the ability to switch an application from one Apple device to another. For example, if you're reading mail on your Apple Watch, you can continue reading the same message on your Mac or iPad. Handoff details are covered in Chapter 8.

1. On your iPhone, open the Apple Watch app.

2. Swipe to scroll to "Settings" and tap "General."

3. Scroll down and touch the "Enable Handoff" switch to toggle it on or off. The switch is green when on and white when off.

3.11 Enable Screenshots

When enabled you can take a screenshot on your Apple Watch. View screenshots in the camera roll on your iPhone. To enable screenshots, follow these steps.

1. On your iPhone, open the Apple Watch app.

2. Swipe to scroll down to "Settings" and tap "General."

3. Scroll down and tap "Enable Screenshots." The slider will turn green when enabled.

Take a Screenshot

Press the side button and hold, and then tap the Digital Crown. The screen flashes to indicate a screenshot was successful. View screenshots on your iPhone in the Photos app.

3.12 What's Next?

The next chapter on watch faces and complications completes the process of customizing your Apple Watch. The chapter wraps up with ideas for sample combinations. For example, for Disney, I use the Mickey Mouse watch face and add the complications for Find

My Friends, Calendar, and Magic Guide to Disney World.

Chapter 3

4. Watch Faces

In this chapter we discuss

Update Your Watch Face

Exploring Interactive Watch Faces

Changing the Watch Face Style

Customizing a Watch Face

The 'My Faces' Screen

Complications

Customized Samples

What's Next?

The beauty of the Apple Watch is that you control which features, apps or app complications appear on your watch face. In this chapter, we will look at how to harness all that power and provide samples of how you can use it in particular situations.

Folks who own high-end timepieces probably recognize the term "complications" when discussing a watch. Any jeweler will tell you that a watch complication is any dial or sub-dial other than the primary display of time on a mechanical watch. Apple Watches are no different from an elegant Swiss watch in that they also use the term complications. Speaking of a Swiss watch, did you know sales of the Apple Watch beat Rolex in 2017?

In this Apple Watch World, individual features of apps are available as complications. I think of complications as little snippets of information. A fitness app might display the number of steps you've taken today in a complication. The Apple Calendar app uses your World Clock time zones as separate complications. For example, once you create a World Clock location for Mumbai and another for New York, you can add both complications to your watch face. As of this writing, 41 complications from Apple are available for the Apple Watch. Not all third-party Apple Watch apps provide complications, but the list of third-party apps with Apple Watch complications is growing daily.

Figure 4.1   The Infographic Watch Face

Apple Watch faces have "template areas" for complications. Where you position a complication on your watch face affects what information is displayed. If the "template area" is relatively small, an icon might be displayed. A larger template area at the bottom of the watch face can display a description of your calendar event. To get you started, I will show you several real-world examples.

The "Utilitarian template" is ideal for displaying data - think stock market, steps, or calories. The Utilitarian template occupies a rectangular area in the top left and right corners of the Utility, Motion, Mickey Mouse and Minnie Mouse watch faces. Utilitarian templates also occupy three corners of the Chronograph watch face and all four corners of the Simple watch face.

The style of the particular watch face may allow you to customize the color, markings or complications in the template areas. You decide which app complications you want in the various template areas. A few Apple app complications are Mail, Messages, or Activity. The addition of third-party app complications like Hotwire or ESPN expand the possibilities for your watch face.

You can choose from 26 basic styles of watch faces that you customize and save in as many combinations as you like. The "My Faces" screen displays your favorite watch faces. Make changes to the "My Faces" selections directly on your watch or within the Apple Watch app on your iPhone.

The "Faces Gallery" displays all the standard Apple Watch Faces. If you delete a watch face from your "My Faces" list, you can always find the watch face again in the "Faces Gallery." The iPhone Apple app also includes a preview option and is generally easier to navigate.

Figure 4.2   The New Toy Story Watch Face

4.1 Update Your Watch Face

1. On your Apple Watch press the Digital Crown to display the Watch Face.

2. Swipe left or right from edge to edge.

3. Stop when you find the watch face you want.

4.2 Exploring Interactive Watch Faces

Depending on the watch face, interactions or animations might be available when you double tap or turn the Digital Crown. These "Easter Eggs" are an unexpected fun surprise. For example, when you double tap the screen, Mickey Mouse announces the time. A few of these Easter Eggs are highlighted in the following section "Customized Samples." For a complete list of watch faces and their respective complications check out the Apple User Guide.

Astronomy

The Astronomy category includes three watch faces: Earth, Moon, and Solar System. Double tap the Solar System watch face to align the planets, or turn the Digital Crown to see the planets move throughout the year. Turning the Digital Crown with the Earth watch face shows the sun moving across the sky, and in the evening hours, the lights in metropolitan areas are visible.

Figure 4.3   The Solar System Watch Face

4.3 Changing the Watch Face Style

You can make multiple versions of any watch face as shown below.

Figure 4.4   Customize the Watch Face

1.   On your Apple Watch, press the Digital Crown to go to the Watch Face.

2.   Firmly press the display.

3.   Swipe all the way to the right, then tap add (the plus symbol.)

4.   Turn the Digital Crown and tap your selected watch face.

1. On your iPhone, open the Apple Watch app.

2. Along the bottom of the screen tap "Face Gallery."

3. Scroll and tap the watch face you want, then tap "Add."

Delete a Watch Face

It is possible to remove watch faces you do not want to show on your Apple Watch. I found all the watch face choices a bit overwhelming so I decided to remove the ones that didn't grab my attention. You can easily add them back if you change your mind. Follow these steps to remove watch faces.

1. On your Apple Watch, press the Digital Crown to go to the Watch Face.

2. Swipe left or right from edge to edge to scroll through watch faces and select the watch face you want to remove.

3. Firmly press the screen and swipe up to remove the watch face.

4.4 Customizing a Watch Face

While editing a watch face, you can customize a highlighted feature. For example, the color of the second hand, or the markings on the face.

1. Press the Digital Crown on your Apple Watch to go to the Watch Face.

2. Firmly press the display and then tap "Customize."

3. Swipe to select the desired feature, for example, the date style.

4. Turn the Digital Crown to change the highlighted feature, for example, the numbers on the dial.

Figure 4.5   Change the Color of the Second Hand

To change your Watch Face on your iPhone, follow these steps.

1. On your iPhone, open the Apple Watch app.

2. In the "My Faces" section, tap the Watch Face.

3. Tap the options for color or style.

4. In "Complications," choose the apps for each option.

5. Scroll down and tap "Set as current Watch Face."

4.5 The 'My Faces' Screen

Think of "My Faces" as your personal, customized watch faces. This is not the same as the "Face Gallery" which is all possible watch faces.

1. On your iPhone, open the Apple Watch app.

2. In the section "My Faces," tap "Edit."

3. Scroll through the gallery to select a watch face.

4. To reorder the list of watch faces, touch the drag icon that looks like 3 horizontal bars on the right. Drag the icon up or down to move the watch face.

5. To remove a watch face from the list, tap the delete button.

Organize Your Watch Faces

1. On your iPhone, open the Apple Watch app.

2. In the "My Faces" section, tap "Edit."

3. Touch and hold the drag icon on the right side of a watch face. The drag icon is three horizontal bars.

4. Drag the watch face up or down to change the list order.

4.6 Complications

Complications on your Watch Face mean your iPhone apps are now part of your Apple Watch face. Apple does a good job of encouraging you to move and exercise all on its own, but adding apps like AllTrails, Big Year Birding, Scavenger or Pokémon introduce a bit of fun into the equation. For example, the "LoseIt!" app reminds me how many calories I should have for lunch. "Notice I didn't say will have but should have." The Pedometer app displays my step counter. Apple has 41 possible complications.

- Activity
- Air Quality
- Alarm
- Battery
- Breathe
- Calendar
- Date
- Digital Time
- Earth
- Favorite Contacts
- Find My Friends
- Heart Rate
- Home
- Mail
- Maps
- Messages
- Monogram
- Moon
- Moon Phase
- Music
- News
- Now Playing
- Phone
- Podcasts
- Radio
- Reminders

- Remote
- Siri
- Solar
- Solar System
- Stocks
- Stopwatch
- Sunrise/Sunset
- Timer
- UV Index
- Walkie-Talkie
- Weather
- Weather Conditions
- Wind
- Workout
- World Clock

First, we will look at the basic steps to add and customize these apps for your watch. Next, we will explore tons of app complications available today, and how to find new apps at any time. For a complete list of the Apple watch faces and their supported Apple complications check out the Apple User Guide.

Select complications for your watch faces using the "Customize" option. Keep in mind that not all apps have complications, and also not all watch faces allow you to add complications.

Add a Complication to Your Watch Face

To change a complication on a watch face, follow these steps.

1. On your Apple Watch, press the Digital Crown to go to the Watch Face.

2. Firmly press the display and then tap "Customize."

3. Swipe to display the highlighted area to customize.

4. Turn the Digital Crown to change the highlighted feature, or select an app "Complication."

The Favorite Complication

The Infograph and Infographic Modular watch faces support adding your "favorite contacts" as a complication.

Add or Remove a Favorite Contact

A favorite contact complication is shown as a letter or photo on your watch face. In this example, the Favorites complication for Michael is shown along the bottom of the screen.

Figure 4.6   The Favorite Complication

1.   On your iPhone, open the "Phone" app.

2.   Tap "Favorites," located in the left corner of the tab bar at the bottom of the screen.

3.   Tap the plus symbol in the top left corner to add a contact.

Remove Complications

Depending on the apps installed on your iPhone, you could have a lot of available complications. That may not be a good thing. For example, I am never going to use the CVS complication on my Apple Watch. Follow the instructions below to remove a complication from your Apple Watch. You can always add it back at in the future.

1. On your iPhone, open the Apple Watch app.

2. Scroll down and tap "Complications."

3. Swipe to delete a complication. Notice the complication is moved to the bottom in the section "Do Not Include."

Complication Not Showing on iPhone

Occasionally I've noticed that a complication won't show as available in the Apple Watch app on the iPhone. However, it is still possible to add the complication on the Apple Watch itself.

1. On your Apple Watch, press the Digital Crown to go to the Watch Face.

2. Firmly press the display and then tap "Customize."

3. Swipe to display the highlighted area to customize.

4. Turn the Digital Crown to change the highlighted feature, or select an app "Complication."

Strangely, the complication will then show in the Apple Watch app on your iPhone, but only for that particular watch face.

Edit Complications

Many app complications work the moment the app is installed, but others do require further setup. For example, Pedometer++ is a third-party app with a "complication" to add steps to your watch face. Before using the complication, you must add Pedometer as a source in the "Health" app.

1. Open the "Health" app on your iPhone.

2. Tap the "Sources" tab, located in the left corner of the tab bar at the bottom of the screen.

3. Scroll down to Pedometer. If you don't see Pedometer in the list of apps, install it on

your iPhone and launch the app at least once.

4.   Tap "Turn All Categories On."

Navigating Complications

In the following example, I have the calendar complication on my watch face.

1.   On your Apple Watch, press the Digital Crown to open your watch face.

2.   Tap the calendar complication.

3.   Turn the Digital Crown to move through days.

Another fun option is the weather complication. Tap to select the weather complication, and turn the Digital Crown to see the hourly forecast, air quality, UV index, wind index, and the 7-day forecast. How cool is that!

4.7 Customized Samples

The following is a gallery showcasing some of the Apple Watch faces. These are organized by interest and include relevant customizations.

Astronomy

The Astronomy watch face category is custom made for astronomy fans. The Astronomy category includes three watch faces.

- Earth
- Moon
- Solar System

Figure 4.7   The Earth Watch Face

Double tap the "Solar System" watch face to align the planets, or turn the Digital Crown to see the planets move throughout the year. In an amazing piece of programming, you can spin the Digital Crown to watch the sun rays move across the "Earth" watch face, and in the evening hours, the lights in metropolitan areas are visible. Apps like "SkyGuide" are also designed for Astronomy fans.

Breathe Watch Face

The Breathe app is available as a watch face in three styles: Focus, Calm, and Classic. When you raise your wrist the watch face guides you through a deep breath. Recent research into the neuroscience of mindfulness shows deep breathing reduces stress and has long-term health benefits.

Color

The simplistic view of the color watch face appeals to me for some reason. With this watch face, it's also easy to scroll through the colors using the Digital Crown.

Figure 4.8   The Color Watch Face

1. On your Apple Watch, press the "Digital Crown" to go to the watch face.

2. Firmly press the display and tap "Customize."

3. Turn the Digital Crown to select a color.

Cooking and Kitchen

When cooking I prefer to tap and swipe on my watch, rather than on my iPhone.

Ideas for Complications:

1. Timer
2. Kitchen Stories
3. Smart Grocery
4. Reminder List (shopping list)
5. Music
6. Siri

Disney

How fun is it to be on vacation at Disney World, and have your own personalized watch face! The Mickey Mouse watch face and new Toy Story watch face are perfect for this adventure. It's also super cool to tap the watch face and have Mickey Mouse announce the time.

1.   Open the Apple Watch app on your iPhone.

2.   Tap "My Watch," located in the left corner of the tab bar at the bottom of the screen.

3.   Scroll down and tap "Sounds & Haptics."

4.   Touch the "Tap to Speak" switch to turn this feature on.

The "Magic Guide to Disney World" app has a complication for the Apple Watch that works with the Mickey Mouse watch face. This app has Disney World wait times, park maps, dining menus, park hours, photos, and more.

Figure 4.9   The Mickey Mouse Watch Face

On my Mickey Mouse watch face, I added Reminders to track my "Disney Fast Pass" selections, as well as Pedometer.

1. Install the Magic Guide to Disney World app on your iPhone.

2. Open the Apple Watch app on your iPhone.

3. Tap "My Watch," located in the left corner of the tab bar at the bottom of the screen.

4. Scroll down and tap "Complications." Make sure "Magic Guide" appears on the list. When done tap "Back."

5. In the "My Faces" section, tap the Mickey Mouse watch face.

6. Scroll down to "Complications" and select the "Magic Guide."

Another complication to consider for Disney is the "Find Friends" app. The "Walkie-Talkie" app is also handy when you're trying to coordinate rides or meals.

Fire, Water, Liquid Metal, and Vapor

The new Vapor, Liquid Metal, Fire and Water motion faces are included with Apple Watch Series 4. On the Apple Watch Series 4 you can set the footage to completely cover the screen from edge-to-edge. These backgrounds are not computer-generated digital effects. The CoolHunting You Tube video, "Apple Watch Series 4 Making of Fire Water and Vapor Faces" is an exclusive behind-the-scenes look into how the videos were created. A high-speed camera captured high-resolution recordings of real fire, water, vapor, and liquid metal.

Kaleidoscope

The Kaleidoscope watch face has infinite possibilities. You select a stock or custom image and choose a style. Turn the Digital Crown to see the kaleidoscope you created.

Figure 4.10   The Kaleidoscope Watch Face

Motion

The motion watch face isn't new with the Series 4 but it is one of those things you just have to try out because it's so fun. There are three collections: butterflies, flowers, and jellyfish. When you firmly press the screen the display cycles through the animations.

Figure 4.11   The Motion Watch Face

Siri

With WatchOS 5, Siri is now an intelligent personal assistant. The Siri watch face monitors your schedule and calendar, suggesting relevant content throughout the day. Intelligent Siri will update you on your favorite team's score, display a photo from a year ago, or recommend a playlist for your commute home. There is also a new option to change the Siri watch face to grey.

Figure 4.12   The Siri Watch Face

1. On your Apple Watch, press the "Digital Crown" to go to the watch face.

2. Firmly press the display and tap "Customize."

3. Turn the Digital Crown to select "Grey" or "Siri Color."

Stocks

The Apple app "Stocks" can display up to 20 stocks and has four complications as shown below. Configure the list of stocks in the iPhone app.

- Current Price
- Points Change
- Percentage Change
- Market Cap

Figure 4.13   Stocks - Market Closed

Timelapse

Displaying location photos throughout the day is an elegant and natural way to indicate the time. The scenes dynamically adjust throughout the day based on time and include these locations.

Figure 4.14 The time-lapse Watch Face

- Mack Lake
- New York
- Hong Kong
- London
- Paris
- Shanghai

World Traveler

Global travelers will appreciate the idea of a world traveler watch face. You customize a watch face to keep track of flight times, hotel reservations, train schedules, car rental, and

Uber ride information. The modular watch face is well suited to this task. If you're visiting one of the locations in the Timelapse collection, you may want to use that watch face.

Leverage these apps when traveling:

- App in the Air
- Babble
- Calendar
- Carrot Weather or Dark Sky
- Citymapper
- ELK (currency converter)
- ETA
- Glympse
- HotWire
- iTranslate
- Weather
- World Clock

To add various world clock complications to your watch face configure them in the clock app.

Configure the World Clock Time Zones

1. On your iPhone, open the "Clock" app.

2. In the bottom left corner of the screen tap "World Clock.

3. Add Mumbai and New York locations.

Add World Clock Complication

1. On your iPhone, open the "Watch" app.

2. Tap a watch face, and then swipe to view complications.

3. Select a time zone.

Figure 4.15   The Activity Digital Watch Face and the World Clock Complication

Your Photo

Each time you raise your wrist, a different photo from your album is displayed on the Photo watch face. First, sync a photo album from your iPhone with your watch.

Create a Photo Album on your iPhone

1. On your iPhone, open the Apple Watch app.

2. Scroll down to "Photos" and select "Synced Album" to select your album.

3. On the main screen, scroll back up to the "My Faces."

4. Tap "Edit" to open the watch face gallery.

4.8 What's Next?

Now that you've configured your Apple Watch exactly the way you want it, it's nice to know your Apple Watch settings are automatically backed up to your iPhone. This is one less task for me to remember. Thank you, Apple!

There is a lot going on at any time on your watch. At times, I feel like I'm bombarded with too much information. The next chapter covers how to customize messages and alert notifications. I will also explain the various app and status icons.

5. Notifications

In this chapter we discuss

Status Icons

Open the Notification Center

Turn App Notifications Off

Change Notification Delivery

Enable Haptic Notifications

Enable the Notification Indicator

Customize App Notifications

Adjust Alert Volume

High or Low Heart Rate Alerts

Troubleshooting Notifications

What's Next?

Once I started gathering all my notes on alerts, status icons, and notifications I realized there are so many they deserve their own chapter. The "Notification Center" is like an inbox for your Apple Watch. The Apple watchOS and various apps are continuously sending messages and alerts to the Notification Center. First, we will look at status icons.

5.1 Status Icons

Status icons communicate information about connections and app activity. Status icons appear in the center section of your watch face along the top edge of the screen. Notifications go to your Apple Watch or your iPhone, but not both. If your iPhone is locked or asleep, you'll get notifications on your Apple Watch.

A blue lock means your watch is locked.

A red dot displayed in the center of your watch face at the top of the screen indicates you have unread notifications. The status icon is configurable as outlined in the following section "Enable the Notification Indicator."

 A red X indicates the Apple Watch has lost connection to the cellular network.

Your Apple Watch isn't connected to your iPhone as indicated by a red iPhone symbol with a slash.

Green dots indicate a connection to a cellular network. The number of dots indicates signal strength.

A green lightning bolt indicates your watch is charging. A red lightning bolt means the battery level is low.

Water lock is active when a blue water drop icon is displayed, indicating your screen is locked. Turn the Digital Crown to turn off water lock.

A purple half-moon symbol means Do Not Disturb is active. The Do Not Disturb status icon on your watch face is a blue moon.

An orange airplane means Airplane Mode is active.

The map symbol is displayed while using the Maps app.

Orange masks indicate Theater Mode is active. Silent Mode is also on. The screen stays dark until you tap the screen or press a button.

A green phone icon indicates a phone call is active.

A purple pointer indicates an app is using location services.

White bars on a red background indicate music is playing.

Tap the yellow walkie-talkie icon to talk to friends instantly.

The runner on a green background indicates a workout is in progress.

5.2 Open the Notification Center

Thanks to watchOS 5 you can open the Control or Notification Center from any screen.

1. On the Apple Watch, touch the top of the screen until a semi-transparent preview of the Notification Center appears, then swipe down.

2. Swipe to the right to confirm or delete the notification.

3. To remove all notifications at once, firmly press the screen and tap "Clear All."

5.3 Turn App Notifications Off

1. On the Apple Watch, touch the top of the watch face until you see the Notification Center, then swipe down.

2. Tap the notification, and swipe to the left.

3. Tap the more icon that looks like an ellipsis or 3 dots.

4. Select "Deliver Quietly" or "Turn off on Apple Watch."

To delete all notifications at once, firmly press the screen and tap "Clear All."

5.4 Change Notification Delivery

You decide how notifications are displayed. The options are "Deliver Quietly" or "Turn off on Apple Watch." Delivery Quietly sends notifications to the "Notification Center" without showing you the alert or delivering a sound or haptic touch. Quiet notifications from the Breathe app immediately go to the Notification Center.

WatchOS 5 now has "grouping" settings for notifications. For example, you can group all "message" notifications or all "email" notifications. Simply tap on the "Messages" stack to see all message notifications. This setting is found in the Watch app on your iPhone.

1.   On the iPhone, open the Apple Watch app.

2.   Tap "Notifications."

3.   Swipe up and tap an app. Swipe up and tap "Notification Grouping," and then tap "By App".

In addition to changing app notification settings in the watch app on your iPhone, you can also change alerts for individual apps on your watch.

1.   On the Apple Watch, touch the top of the watch face, then swipe down.

2.   Swipe left on a notification, then tap "More" (the ellipsis icon).

3.   Tap "Deliver Quietly" or "Turn off on Apple Watch."

4.   To see or hear notifications again tap "Deliver Prominently."

Tip: When an annoying group chat is constantly sending notifications to your watch, turning on "Deliver Quietly" for that app is a simple way to quietly deliver only those alerts to notification center. Your other notifications will continue to alert you. Reverse the process to receive notifications from that app again.

5.5 Enable Haptic Notifications

Haptics also play a role in alerts. For example, the Map app gently vibrates to indicate an upcoming turn. This is a useful accessibility feature for deaf or hard of hearing drivers.

1.   On your iPhone, open the Apple Watch app.

2.   In the "Sounds & Haptics" section, tap the "Haptic Alerts" to toggle on or off. The switch is green when on and white when off.

Change the haptic alert strength to "Prominent" in this section.

5.6 Enable the Notification Indicator

A red dot displayed in the center of your watch face at the top of the screen indicates you have unread notifications.

1. On the iPhone, open the Apple Watch app.

2. Tap "Notifications."

3. Enable "Notifications Indicator." When enabled a red dot at the top of your watch face indicates you have unread notifications.

5.7 Customize App Notifications

Some apps allow you to customize notification options. There is also a choice to "Mirror my iPhone" to use the same notification settings on your iPhone and Apple Watch. There are three settings for notifications.

- Allow Notifications
- Send to Notification Center
- Notifications Off

To set app notification options follow these steps.

1. On the iPhone, open the Apple Watch app.

2. Tap "Notifications."

3. Swipe up and tap an app, and then select the option.

Mail Notifications

In addition to notifications for each of your email accounts, you can set preview and other options in the Mail settings. For example, if you tap the "VIP" option, you will only get an alert when you receive an email from someone you've marked as important.

1. Open the Apple Watch app on your iPhone.

2. Tap "My Watch," located in the left corner of the tab bar at the bottom of the screen.

3. Scroll down and tap "Mail."

4. Tap "Allow Notifications."

Set Mail VIPs

1. On your iPhone, open the Mail app.

2. In the section mailboxes, tap VIP.

3. Select a contact, then tap VIP Alerts, and toggle "Allow Notifications" on.

4. Open the Apple Watch app on your iPhone.

5. Tap "My Watch," located in the left corner of the tab bar at the bottom of the screen.

6. Swipe and tap Notifications.

7. Scroll and tap "Mail."

8. Tap "VIPs" and choose Sound or Haptic alerts.

Map Notifications

The gentle haptic (wrist tap) notifications are invaluable when navigating with Maps. Navigation "Turn Alerts" are configurable in the Apple Watch app. If you'd also like haptic alerts, enable those under Sounds & Haptics as shown earlier.

1.   On your iPhone, open the Apple Watch app.

2.   Tap "Notifications."

3.   Swipe up and tap "Maps."

4.   Tap the toggle switch for "Driving," "Driving with CarPlay," or "Walking." The switch is green when on and white when off.

Message Notifications

Message notifications are configurable for individual contacts. If you don't want to receive message notifications on your watch enable "Hide Alerts" for that contact.

1.   On your iPhone, open a message from John.

2.   At the top of the screen tap "Info."

3.   Swipe up and tap "Hide Alerts" to enable hide alerts.

A "Do Not Disturb" icon will appear on the left side of the message indicating notifications are off. Repeat steps 1-3 to disable "Hide Alerts."

Troubleshooting Message Notifications

There are a few things to check when you are not receiving message notifications.

1. In the Apple Watch app on your iPhone check if the setting "Mirror My iPhone" is enabled. In the Watch app open "Notifications" and then tap "Messages."

2. On your iPhone disable "Allow Notifications" and force restart your iPhone. Enable "Allow Notifications." Try turning on "Badge App Icon" and "Show on Lock Screen."

3. Check if "Mute" or "Do Not Disturb" is enabled.

4. Unlock your watch screen.

5. Force restart your watch. Press the side button and Digital Crown for three seconds until the Apple logo appears.

6. Check connectivity. Swipe up on your watch face to open the Control Panel.

7. Check your settings for iMessage. iMessage allows you to send to an email address if that contact has an Apple device. On your iPhone in "Settings" open "Messages." In the section "Send &

Receive" verify your Apple ID and SMS phone number.

8. A basic test involves sending a test SMS message by typing in a phone number in the "To" section of the message.

Workout Reminders

The Apple Watch Series 4 will automatically detect certain types of workouts like running or walking. To enable this feature use the Apple Watch app on your iPhone.

1. On your iPhone, open the Apple Watch app.

2. Tap "My Watch," located in the left corner of the tab bar along the bottom of the screen.

3. Tap the toggle switch for "Start Workout Reminder" and "End Workout Reminder." The switch is green when on and white when off.

Calendar Notifications

Calendar notifications are customizable, depending on the type of event and notification method. Notification methods are either "sound" or "haptic."

1. On your iPhone, open the Apple Watch app.

2. Swipe up and tap on "Calendar."

3. Scroll down and tap one of the options: Upcoming Events, Invitations, Invitee Responses, Shared Calendar Alerts.

5.8 Adjust Alert Volume

1. On your Apple Watch, press the Side Button.

2. Swipe and tap "Settings."

3. Scroll down and tap "Sounds & Haptics."

4. Move the slider bar to adjust volume.

5.9 High or Low Heart Rate Alerts

The Apple Watch Series 4 has a new set of features that warn you if your heart rate is higher or lower than usual. Your watch compares data with your average heart rate to identify temporary changes. Check out the "Heart Rate" app in Chapter 6 for instructions on how to view your "Heart Rate Recovery."

1. On your iPhone, open the Apple Watch app.

2. Tap "Notifications."

3. Tap "High Heart Rate" or "Low Heart Rate" and set the threshold.

5.10 Troubleshooting Notifications

If you don't see notifications, check your paired iPhone is connected and the Apple Watch is not locked.

1. On your Apple Watch, press the Digital Crown to open the Home screen.

2. Swipe up from the bottom of the screen to open the Control Center.

3. In the top left corner, verify the companion iPhone status icon is green.

4. Ensure Wi-Fi is enabled.

5. Make sure "Do Not Disturb" is disabled.

5.11 What's Next?

Chapters 2 through 5 covered the logistics and configuration of the Apple Watch. Now it's time to look at the apps, and explore what the Apple Watch can do on a daily basis.

Chapter 5

6. Watch Apps

In this chapter we discuss

There are two kinds of apps, Apple apps, and third-party apps. Not all iPhone apps will work on your Apple Watch. Apps displayed in the Apple Watch app on your iPhone are fully compatible with your Apple Watch. While you can install apps through the regular iPhone App Store, when browsing for new apps it's a good idea to use the Apple Watch app to ensure compatibility. If you've been searching for a watch app to no avail, chances are there is already an IFTTT applet that does what you need, as outlined in Chapter 7.

6.1 Installing Apps on your Apple Watch

Existing compatible iPhone apps are listed in the "Available Apps" section of the Apple Watch app. You can search for new apps with either the "App Store" or "Search" buttons. Both options are outlined in the next section.

Add an Existing iPhone App

If you did not enable the option for automatic app install, as outlined by the topic "General Settings" in Chapter 3, follow these steps to install an app on your watch.

1. Open the Apple Watch app on your iPhone.

2. Tap "My Watch," located in the left corner of the tab bar at the bottom of the screen.

3. Swipe to scroll down to the section "Available Apps." Tap the app you would like to add.

4. Swipe left to delete an app.

Search for Apps to Install

To find a new app in the Apple Watch app on your iPhone, tap "App Store" or "Search" in the tab bar along the bottom of the screen.

Remove Apps

Personally, I like to have a firm handle on what apps are on my Apple Watch or iPhone. App syncing between your watch and iPhone drains the battery. Unused apps waste valuable storage space. Chapter 11 includes instructions to check storage space.

1.   Open the Apple Watch app on your iPhone.

2.   In the section "Installed on Apple Watch," tap the app you want to remove.

3.   Ensure "Show App on Apple Watch" is not enabled. The slide bar should be white.

Tip: If you remove an app from your iPhone, it is automatically removed from your Apple Watch.

Remove Apps Using iPhone Storage

The iPhone Storage screen provides a quick way to remove several apps. The "iPhone storage" list view lists all installed apps. The view includes the app size and last used date. I suspect it displays "Never Used" when you download a new version of an app because I know I use my YMCA app all the time, but it's usually marked "Never Used." I've learned to be careful when removing apps.

1. On your iPhone, open Settings and tap "General."

2. Scroll down and tap "iPhone Storage."

3. Tap the app you want to remove, then tap "Delete App."

6.2 Alarms

It's pretty easy to add or delete an alarm on your Apple Watch. You can add the complication for Alarms to your watch face as outlined in Chapter 4.

Add an Alarm

1. On your Apple Watch press the side button to open The Dock.

2. Swipe to scroll and tap the "Alarms" app.

3. Tap "Add alarm."

4. Turn the Digital Crown to adjust the alarm time.

5. Tap "Set."

6. Tap the new alarm to set options for repeat or to change the alarm name.

Delete an Alarm

1. On your Apple Watch, tap the alarm.

2. Swipe to scroll down.

3. Tap Delete.

6.3 Apple Pay & the Wallet App

Apple Pay is integrated with the Apple Wallet App. I probably went overboard with examples in this section, but it's not my fault you can use Apple Pay in so many ways!

First, we'll look at what's in your wallet. Next, I explain how to use your watch with Apple Pay and Siri in messages, at a store, or how to confirm a transaction in Safari on your Mac. There are five examples of adding third-party app cards and reservations (Fandango, Hilton, Marriott, Sephora, and Starbucks.) Next, we'll look at how to add any card, ticket, or pass that has a bar code to your wallet using the "Pass2U" app.

Funds for Apple Pay come from credit cards or Apple Pay Cash stored in the Apple "Wallet" app. The "Wallet" app houses this information:

- Hotel Reservations
- Credit Cards
- Membership Cards
- Airline Boarding Passes
- Movie Tickets
- Coupons
- Transit Cards
- Student IDs
- Tickets

Figure 6.1   The Apple Wallet App

There are several ways to use Apple Pay with your Apple Watch as outlined in the detailed examples that follow.

- Ask Siri to send cash in a message.

- Confirm a Safari transaction with your watch.

- Pay a store merchant using your watch.

For example, at Subway, you click the side button on your watch twice to pay the merchant.

Ask Siri to Send Cash in a Message

Apple Pay is integrated with SiriKit. On your Apple Watch ask Siri to "Pay Michael one dollar," and Siri does the rest.

Figure 6.2   Sending Cash in a Message with Apple Pay

Safari Apple Pay and Apple Watch

On Apple devices, you can also use Apple Pay in Safari. Start the transaction in the Safari web browser, and when prompted "confirm" the payment on your Apple Watch.

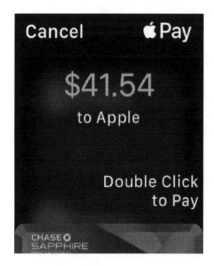

Figure 6.3   Confirm Safari Apple Pay Transaction

Pay a Merchant on Your Watch

To initiate an Apple Pay transaction, the merchant activates Apple Pay on their payment terminal. Next, you press the side button on your Apple Watch twice.

Tip: Apple Pay is unavailable if you turn off passcode.

1. Open the Apple Watch app on your iPhone.

2. Tap "My Watch," located in the left corner of the tab bar along the bottom of the screen.

3. Scroll down to "Passcode."

Add Cards and Passes to Apple Wallet

Third-party apps that support the Apple Wallet PassKit framework include a button to "Add to Apple Wallet," as shown in Figure 6.4.

Figure 6.4   Add to Apple Wallet Logo

The instructions for adding third-party cards to the Wallet app vary depending on the particular third-party app, so I've provided a few examples below. The Marriott example includes adding both the Marriott Rewards card, as well as a particular hotel reservation.

- Fandango
- Hilton

- Marriott
- Sephora
- Starbucks

Once a third-party app is installed on your iPhone or Apple Watch, look for an option to add the card or pass to Apple Wallet. The following examples demonstrate the steps, although they vary slightly.

Starbucks: Launch the Starbucks app, select Manage, Details, and click "Add to Apple Wallet."

Hilton Honors: Launch the Hilton app, select Stays, Upcoming, and click "Add to Apple Wallet."

Marriott: Launch the Marriott app and select "My Account." Swipe up and tap "Add to Apple Wallet." To add a reservation tap the menu icon to see your reservations. Tap the confirmation number, and then click "Add to Apple Wallet."

Sephora: Open the Sephora app and click on Beauty Insider. Click "Add to Apple Wallet."

Fandango: Open the Fandango app and go to "Account." Select "Purchases," swipe up and tap "Purchase Details." Click "Add to Apple Wallet."

Another option to add cards to your Wallet is to scan a QR code to add a card.

1. Open the Wallet app on your iPhone.

2. Tap "Edit Passes."

3. Tap "Find Apps for Wallet" or "Scan code."

When scanning codes the Apple Wallet app launches the camera and displays a square finder marquee to select a "QR code." The Apple PassKit framework supports 128 QR Codes. To add tickets or passes with a bar code, that do not have direct integration with Apple Wallet, use a third-party app like "Pass2U."

Add Bar Code Tickets with Pass2U

There are probably several third-party apps that create QR codes for your Apple Wallet, but I use "Pass2U." In Figure 6.5 you can see a ticket for the Atlanta Symphony in my Apple Wallet. I scanned the bar code on the original ticket into the "Pass2U" app, added a logo photo, location, time, and seat.

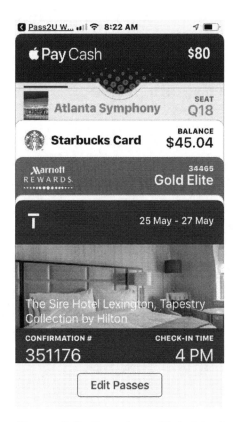

Figure 6.5 Symphony Ticket in Apple Wallet

After clicking "Add," the new ticket is shown in my Apple Wallet.

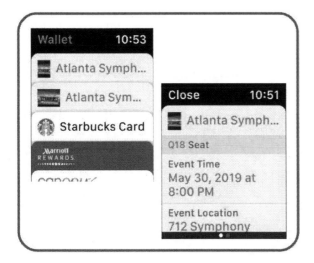

Figure 6.6   The Wallet App on Your Watch

Activate Credit Cards on Your Watch

Although you may have credit cards set up in Apple Pay, you must activate the card on your Apple Watch. Enter the corresponding card security code in your Apple Watch app on your iPhone to activate the card. Student IDs require the eAccounts and Duo Mobile apps.

Reorder Cards in the Wallet

To reorder cards touch the card in the Wallet app and drag it up or down to change the order. This is also how you set the default card.

Transit Cards

In Japan the Tokyo transit Suica card works with Apple Pay. When Suica is set as your Express Transit Card, simply hold your watch close to the ticket gate scanner. There is no need to wake or unlock your watch. In Beijing and Shanghai, you can also use transit cards; just make sure your region is China in "Settings" on your watch and iPhone as outlined in Chapter 3.

Status of the Apple Pay System

It is possible that the Apple Pay system is down for maintenance. You can check the Apple Pay system status at https://www.apple.com/support/systemstatus/.

6.4 Calendars and Reminders

The Apple Calendar is the simplest way to display your schedule on your Apple Watch.

1. On your Apple Watch open the calendar app.

2. Firmly press the screen to see the options "Up Next," "List" or "Today" to change the calendar view.

3. Tap to select an event, firmly press the screen to see the option for "Directions."

Display Month View

1. On your Apple Watch open the calendar app.

2. Tap the top left corner of the screen to change views. Swipe to scroll through days.

Add an Event

Use the calendar app on your iPhone to add an event to your calendar.

If you've enabled "handoff," you can quickly switch to the calendar app on your iPhone. Unlock your iPhone and tap the banner, along the bottom of the screen, to open the calendar app on your iPhone. Enable handoff in the Apple

Watch app in the "General" settings screen, as shown in Chapter 3.

Customize Notifications

Calendar notifications are customizable depending on the type of event, as well as the notification method: "sound" or "haptic." Notifications are discussed in detail in Chapter 5.

1. On your iPhone, open the Apple Watch app.

2. Swipe up and tap on Calendar.

3. Scroll down and tap one of the notification options: Upcoming Events, Invitations, Invitee Responses, or Shared Calendar Alerts.

Integration with Third-Party Calendar Apps

There are several integration options for third-party calendar accounts.

146

- Use a third-party app like Tiny Calendar.

- Add your other calendar account to your iPhone calendar app as shown below.

- Setup the other calendar app to send alerts to your iPhone. Every time you create an appointment set a reminder.

Add Accounts to Apple Calendar on Your iPhone

1. On your iPhone, go to "Settings."

2. Scroll down to "Passwords & Accounts."

3. In the "Accounts" section, tap "Add Account."

4. Select Google and follow the login prompts. If you have trouble connecting your Google account, log in to your Google account from a web browser and follow the prompts to set up an App password.

Add Accounts to Apple Calendar on Your Mac

You can also add a Google calendar to your Mac calendar, and then it will be available to your Apple Watch.

1. On your Mac, launch your calendar.

2. On the "Calendar" menu, select "Preferences."

3. On the "Accounts" tab, click the plus symbol in the bottom left corner of the window to add your Google account.

Sync Issues

When your contacts or calendar are not syncing properly try a reset.

1. On the iPhone, open the Apple Watch app.

2. Tap "My Watch," located in the left corner of the tab bar at the bottom of the screen.

3. Tap "General" and then tap "Reset."

4. Tap "Reset Sync Data."

6.5 Camera Remote

You're probably thinking, "the Apple Watch doesn't have a camera," and that's true. However, the Apple Watch makes a great remote control. In addition to Apple's "Camera Remote" app, third-party apps like ProCamera, Hydra, and Camera Plus enhance camera remote control features.

Camera Remote and Timer

Position your iPhone to take a photo, then use the "Camera Remote" app on your Apple Watch to view a preview and take a photo. Note that your Apple Watch must be within 33 feet or 10 meters of your iPhone.

1. On your Apple Watch open the "Camera Remote" app.

2. Position your iPhone to frame the shot, using your Apple Watch as a viewfinder.

3. Tap the "Shutter" button.

Review Photos

1. Tap the thumbnail in the bottom left corner of the screen to view your photos.

2. Swipe left or right.

3. Turn the Digital Crown to zoom.

4. Touch the screen and drag your finger to pan.

5. Tap the screen to close.

6.6 Clock

The Clock app on your iPhone has an option for "World Clock" where you create "time zones." Each time zone you create can be used as a separate complication for your watch face.

Figure 6.7   World Clock

Configure the World Clock Time Zones

1. On your iPhone, open the "Clock" app.

2. Tap "World Clock" located in the left corner of the tab bar at the bottom of the screen.

3. Add Mumbai and New York locations.

Add the World Clock Complication

1. On your iPhone, open the "Watch" app.

2. Tap a watch face, and then swipe to view complications.

3. Select a World Clock complication.

Figure 6.8   Time Zones

Monogram

The clock monogram can include up to 5 characters. The monogram is shown in the center of your watch face.

1. On your iPhone, open the Apple Watch app.

2. Scroll down and tap "Clock."

3. Tap "Monogram" and choose up to 5 letters.

6.7 Emergency SOS and Medical ID

Medical ID and SOS information are displayed on your Apple Watch screen when the side button is pressed for three seconds.

Apple Watch Series 4 uses the accelerometer and gyroscope to detect a significant, hard fall. When your watch detects a hard fall, it taps you on the wrist, sounds an alarm, and displays an alert. You can choose to contact emergency services or dismiss the alert by tapping "I fell, but I'm OK," or by scrolling down and tapping "I did not fall."

Figure 6.9   The Hard Fall Alert

Configure Medical ID in the Health App

1.   On your iPhone, open the "Health" app.

2.   Tap "Medical ID" located in the right corner of the tab bar at the bottom of the screen.

3.   Enter your information.

Configure Emergency SOS

1.   On your iPhone, open the Apple Watch App.

2.   Tap "Emergency SOS."

3.   Enter your information.

View Medical ID or Call Emergency Services

When anyone holds the side button on your watch for 3 seconds, your Apple Watch will call Emergency Services. The Apple Watch counts down with an alarm, and a slider prompts if you want to end the call. Also, this option automatically detects if you take a hard fall. If you don't respond, it will tap your wrist, sound an alarm, and then call emergency services.

1. On your Apple Watch press and hold the side button until the screen opens.

2. Tap Medical ID or Emergency SOS.

Enable Emergency SOS

1. Open the Apple Watch app on your iPhone.

2. Tap "My Watch," located in the left corner of the tab bar at the bottom of the screen.

3. Scroll down to "Emergency SOS."

4. Touch the "Emergency SOS" slider. Continue holding the slider as you move it to enabled. The slider is green when enabled and white when disabled.

6.8 Find Friends

The complication for the "Find my Friends" is one of the more advanced in terms of features. It shows where your friends are

Chapter 6

with a timestamp. A great security feature for teenagers, it's also handy when you're at a theme park, trying to coordinate rides or meals.

To add friends to the list add them in the app on your iPhone.

1. On your iPhone, open the "Find Friends" app.

2. In the "My Faces" section tap the Watch Face.

3. Tap "Add" to invite friends.

4. On your Apple Watch press the "Digital Crown" to open the Dock. If you don't see the Find Friends app, follow the instructions for adding apps to the Dock in Chapter 2.

5. Tap the "Find Friends" app.

6. Tap the name of your friend. The time, location, and map of your friend's last known location are shown.

Get Location Notifications

Have you ever wondered if your spouse has left work yet? I don't want to seem like a stalker

156

and nag my husband to tell me when he's left work, but it's nice to know it's time to put dinner in the oven. The "Find My Friends" app has this eventuality covered. In the following example, I set up a notification when my spouse leaves a particular location, in this case work.

1. On your iPhone, open the "Find My Friends" app.

2. Tap the friend you want to track.

3. Tap "Notify Me." Ensure you've selected the choice "The next time Michael: Leaves."

4. Tap "Other" and browse to select a location. Tap "Done" to create the notification.

5. Tap "More..." and then tap "Choose Label" and then tap "Custom Label." Type a name for the label.

6.9 The Heart Rate App

The Heart Rate app displays your current, resting, and walking average heart rate. When you open the Heart Rate app on your watch it measures your heart rate every five seconds. To measure your heart rate every second, touch your finger to the Digital Crown. When you lift your finger the Heart Rate app goes back to measuring your heart rate every five seconds.

1.   On your Apple Watch, press the Side Button.

2.   Scroll and tap the "Heart Rate" app.

3.   Swipe or turn the Digital Crown to see your "Resting Rate" and your "Walking Average" heart rate.

Heart Rate Recovery

The Heart Rate app also records your Heart Rate Recovery after a workout. Heart Rate Recovery was introduced in watchOS 4. Heart Rate Recovery measures your heart rate when you end a workout, and compares it to your heart rate two minutes later. So for instance, depending on your age, a heart rate recovery over 60 would be considered very good. Search the internet for the latest information on heart rate recovery and see where you stand. There is scientific evidence that suggests a low heart rate recovery indicates heart problems.

1. After a workout, on your Apple Watch press the side button.

2. Swipe and tap "Heart Rate" to open the Heart Rate app.

3. Swipe up to view your "Recovery Rate."

View Heart Rate Data

The Health Data tab is also where you can view data from the "Heart Rate" app.

1. On your iPhone, open the "Health" app.

2. In the bottom tab bar tap "Health Data."

3. Swipe up and tap "Heart."

4. Tap the arrows at the top of the screen to move between days. Tap again to change to hour, day, week, month, or year view. Tap anywhere on the graph to view the day, time, minimum, and maximum information.

6.10 The Home App

With "Home" app versions for your smartphone, MAC, tablet and Apple Watch it is very convenient to control your smart home devices. Rooms and devices set as "Favorites" automatically appear in the Apple Watch "Home" app.

Configure Rooms and Devices for Apple Watch

1. Open the "Home" app on your tablet, smartphone or MAC.

2. Double click, or firmly press, on a room. Click on "Settings."

3. Ensure the toggle "Include in Favorites" is turned on.

4. Open the "Home" app on your Apple Watch and swipe to control rooms and devices.

6.11 Keynote

Keynote presentations are easily controlled with your Apple Watch, although there are a few settings that will ensure things work smoothly.

1. On your Apple Watch, press the side button to open the Dock.

2. Tap "Settings."

3. Tap "General," then tap "Wake Screen."

4. Turn on "Wake Screen on Wrist Raise."

5. Under "Resume To," select "Previous Activity."

6.12 Mail

In addition to reading mail, you can reply, delete, flag, or mark a message unread.

Read and Reply to an email

1. On your Apple Watch press the Digital Crown.

2. Swipe and tap "Mail."

3. Swipe to scroll, or turn the Digital Crown.

4. Tap to read the message.

5. Swipe up and tap "Reply."

To see additional options like delete, firmly press the screen while the message is displayed.

Mail Settings - Inboxes

1. On your iPhone, open the "Apple Watch" app.

2. Swipe and tap "Mail."

3. In the section "Mail Settings" tap "Include Mail."

4. Tap the accounts you want to include.

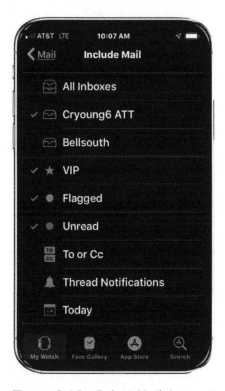

Figure 6.10   Select Mail Accounts

Delete an Email

To delete an email in your inbox, tap and swipe left .

Flag Style

Use the Apple Watch app to set the style for mail flags.

1. Open the Apple Watch app on your iPhone.

2. Tap "My Watch," located in the left corner of the tab bar at the bottom of the screen.

3. Scroll down and tap "Mail."

4. Tap "Custom."

5. Swipe down and select the "Flag Style" color or shape.

Set Mail Options

In addition to notifications for each of your email accounts, you can set preview and other options in the mail settings. For example, the "VIP" option ensures you are alerted only when you receive an email from someone you've marked as important.

1. Open the Apple Watch app on your iPhone.

2. Tap "My Watch," located in the left corner of the tab bar at the bottom of the screen.

3. Scroll down and tap "Mail."

4. Tap "Allow Notifications."

Set VIPs

1. On your iPhone, open the Mail app.

2. In the section "mailboxes," tap VIP.

3. Select a contact, then tap "VIP Alerts." Toggle "Allow Notifications" on.

4. Open the Apple Watch app on your iPhone.

5. Tap "My Watch," located in the left corner of the tab bar at the bottom of the screen.

6. Swipe and tap "Notifications."

7. Scroll and tap "Mail."

8. Tap "VIPs" and choose Sound or Haptic alerts.

6.13 Maps

Your Apple Watch can display maps, the location of friends in the "Find Friends" app, and provide navigation directions. For example, the app uses haptics to gently vibrate to indicate an upcoming turn.

Tip: Recent locations are shown when you swipe up on your watch face.

Navigation

On your Apple Watch, press the side button, swipe, and tap "Maps." Tap "Location" and then turn the Digital Crown to zoom in and out.

Map Notifications

Navigation "Turn Alerts" are configurable in the Apple Watch app.

1. On your iPhone, open the Apple Watch app.

2. Tap "Notifications."

3. Swipe up and tap "Maps."

4. Tap the toggle switch for "Driving," "Driving with CarPlay," or "Walking." A switch is green when on and white when off.

Find an Address for a Contact

To find a contact address, open a map on your Apple Watch, firmly press the display, tap "Search Here," tap Contacts, turn the Digital Crown to scroll, then tap the contact. If the contact information includes an address, you can select walking or driving directions.

'Search Here' and 'Transit Map'

1. On your Apple Watch, press the Side Button to open the Dock.

2. Tap the 'Maps' app.

3. Select a map location.

4. Firmly press the screen.

5. Select "Transmit Map" or "Search Here." The search options include dictation, scribble, and contacts.

6. When searching, swipe up to select nearby options such as food, drinks, shopping, travel, services, fun, health, or transport.

7. For directions to a particular location, tap the location, then scroll down and choose walking, driving, or bus.

8. Turn the Digital Crown to pan or zoom on the map. To add a pin, tap the map and hold till you see a pin, then release. Tap the pin to see the address information.

6.14 Messages, Digital Touch, & Apple Pay

The Apple messaging app supports dictating traditional text messages, audio clips, emoticons, tap backs (handy phrases), sending money with Apple pay, scribble, and sharing a map of your location. At any point, you can firmly press the display to call or email your friend.

Digital Touch is a fun way to include animation or sketches in your messages. Digital touch is only available if the recipient also has an Apple device.

Create a Message

1. Press the Side Button on your Apple Watch to open the Dock.

2. Swipe the screen with your finger, or turn the Digital Crown.

3. Tap on the "Messages" app.

4. Firmly press the screen and tap "New Message."

5.   Choose a contact, enter a phone number, or dictate a phone number.

6.   Touch anywhere on the screen to send the message.

Read a Message

Turn the Digital Crown to scroll through a message. To quickly return to the first message tap your friend's name at the top of the screen. Turn the Digital Crown to see previous messages from that contact. Firmly press the screen to see options.

- Reply
- Details
- Send Location
- Choose Language

To delete a message select the message in your inbox and swipe left. Click on the trash can symbol.

Reply to a Message

Turn the Digital Crown to scroll to the bottom of the message, then tap one of the icons to reply. Tap the microphone to dictate your response.

Scroll past the icons to the end to respond with a "Tap Back." Touch "Tap Back" and choose one of the responses.

Emojis are tiny symbols. In addition to emojis, you can reply with a sticker. Stickers include handwritten responses. Tap the emoji icon, swipe, and tap "Stickers."

Tip: Animated Emojis are not available on Apple Watch Series 4.

Scribble

Scribble a quick note if the built-in responses aren't appropriate. For example, if you're in a meeting and your daughter asks you to meet for lunch; you can reply "OK," and then scribble a time like "12." Tap "Scribble" and then write your message. As you write, turn the Digital Crown to see predictive text options, then tap one to choose it. Tap "Send" to send the message.

Dictate

Tap the microphone icon , dictate your message, then tap "Done." You can also verbally add punctuation. For example, "Did it arrive question mark."

Create an Audio Clip

To change a text message to an audio clip, follow these steps.

1. Open the Apple Watch app on your iPhone and tap "My Watch."

2. Swipe and tap on "Messages."

3. Tap "Dictated Messages," then tap Transcript or Audio.

The Default Type of Audio Response

1. Open the Apple Watch app on your iPhone. Tap "My Watch," located in the left corner of the tab bar at the bottom of the screen.

2. Tap "Messages," and then tap "Dictated Messages Transcript."

3. Choose from "Transcript," "Audio," or "Transcript or Audio."

View a Message Timestamp

To see when a message was sent while reading the message swipe left.

Options

Force touch the screen to view the message options. The "Details" option displays contact information. The "Details" has choices to phone, text or email the contact.

- Reply
- Details
- Send Location
- Choose Language

Smart Replies

Apple provides a customizable list of handy phrases, sometimes referred to as "tap backs."

1. Open the Apple Watch app on your iPhone and tap My Watch.

2. Swipe up, tap "Messages," then tap "Default Replies." Tap "Add Reply."

3. To reorder the default replies, tap "Edit." To reorder replies, drag the icon on the right that looks like 3 horizontal bars.

4. To delete a smart reply, touch, and swipe to the left. You can also tap the red minus symbol.

Message Alerts

Message alerts can be set to repeat never, once, twice, three times, five times, or even ten times.

Use Apple Pay to Send & Receive $

With Apple Pay, you can send or receive money. Apple Pay is available on your Apple Watch if you've enabled "Apple Pay Cash" in your Apple Wallet app on your iPhone. If you've added "cash" to your account, you can send cash to friends or family in a message.

1. On your Apple Watch, press the Digital Crown.

2. Swipe and tap "Messages."

3. Start a new conversation, or continue an existing conversation.

4. Tap the icon for Apple Pay.

5. Select an amount to send using the plus or minus symbol, or turn the Digital Crown.

6. Tap "Pay."

7. Double-click the side button to send.

Digital Touch

When you send friends a digital touch message, they also receive a haptic (wrist tap) response. This is a new take on the idea of reaching out and touching someone.

1. On your Apple Watch, press the Digital Crown.

2. Swipe and then tap "Messages."

3. Start a new conversation or continue an existing conversation.

4. Tap the icon for Digital Touch.

To Show Emotion Try These Digital Touch Options.

Send a Kiss: Tap two fingers on the screen.

Send your Heartbeat: Touch two fingers to the screen until you see and feel your heartbeat.

Break a Heart: Touch two fingers to the screen until you see and feel your heartbeat, then drag down.

Show anger: Touch and hold one finger on the display till you see a flame.

Sketch: Draw on the screen.

6.15 Music

With the Apple music app, you can listen to songs, albums, playlists, or artists. There are two options for playing music: either stream music over cellular or download music to your watch.

Reproduce Chapter 6

Play Music

1. On your Apple Watch, press the Digital Crown.

2. Swipe and tap "Music."

3. Swipe up, or turn the Digital Crown.

4. Tap "On iPhone," "Shuffle All," or "Library."

5. Swipe and tap to select Playlists, Artists, Albums, or Songs.

6. Tap the song to play.

Add a Workout Playlist

Whenever you start a workout, you can automatically play music from a workout playlist. Configure the playlist in the Apple watch app on your iPhone.

1. On your iPhone, open the Apple Watch app.

2. Swipe to scroll down and tap "Workout."

3. Swipe up and tap "Workout playlist" to select a playlist for your workouts.

Use Audio Output With Apple Watch

To stream music or videos to your favorite speakers, AirPods, or headsets, use the Control Center.

1. Swipe up on the Apple Watch face to open Control Center.

2. Tap the "Audio Output" icon.

Tapping the audio output icon will also switch audio output between paired Bluetooth devices.

Shuffle, Repeat, Source and Output

When playing music, firmly press the screen to view these options.

- Shuffle
- Repeat
- Source
- Output

Change Volume With the Digital Crown

Tap the audio  status icon on your watch face and turn the Digital Crown to adjust volume. Control music, podcasts, or hearing aid volume. If you have Bluetooth speakers or a headset connected to your Apple Watch, this is a simple way to adjust the volume.

Figure 6.11   Change Volume

Download Music to Your Apple Watch

To listen to music on the go when you don't have your iPhone with you, download albums or playlists to your Apple watch. If you subscribe to Apple Music, the "Favorites Mix" and "New Music Mix" are automatically added.

1. On your iPhone, open the Apple Watch app.

2. Tap "My Watch," located in the left corner of the tab bar at the bottom of the screen.

3. Swipe to scroll down and tap "Music."

4. Tap "Add Music" and then tap the playlist or album you want to add. This is also where you could delete a playlist.

5. To download music connect your watch to Power and place it near your iPhone.

Check Available Space

Music files can use up a lot of storage space. In case you're wondering how much space is used, on your iPhone open the Apple Watch app to see detailed information.

- The count of songs on your watch.

- The count of photos on your watch.

- The number of applications on your watch.

- The total capacity.

- The available capacity.

1. On your iPhone, open the Apple Watch app.

2. Tap "My Watch," located in the left corner of the tab bar at the bottom of the screen.

3. Swipe to scroll down and tap "General."

4. Tap "About" to see available capacity.

6.16 Phone

The "Phone" app on your Apple Watch controls phone calls. With the cellular option on your Apple Watch, you don't need your companion iPhone nearby. The Phone app includes these features.

- Favorites
- Recents
- Contacts
- Keypad
- Voice mail

Make a Call

1. Press the Side Button on your Apple Watch to open the Dock.

2. Swipe the screen with your finger, or turn the Digital Crown.

3. Tap on the "Phone" app.

4. Firmly press the screen and tap "New Call."

5. Tap "keypad," enter the number, then tap the phone symbol.

Emergency Phone Call

Press and hold the Side Button on your Apple Watch to make an emergency phone call. Enable Emergency Services, set your Medical ID, and configure SOS settings on your iPhone as outlined earlier.

Answer a Call

To answer a call tap the green "Phone" icon. To see additional options, turn the Digital Crown or swipe up on the screen.

- Answer on iPhone
- Send a Message

During a call swipe up to see options or activate the keypad.

- Mute
- Volume
- Keypad

Decline a Call

To decline an incoming call, double tap the Digital Crown. Another option is to tap the red phone icon. The call is sent to voice mail.

Transfer a Call to Your iPhone

Thanks to Apple's "Continuity" platform, you can easily handoff a call from your Apple Watch to your iPhone.

1. On your Apple Watch, swipe up on the screen when receiving an incoming call.

2. Tap "Answer on iPhone" to place the call on hold.

3. On your iPhone, swipe up on the phone symbol located in the bottom left corner of the iPhone lock screen.

After answering a call on your watch, at any time you can tap the banner on your iPhone, to switch the call to your iPhone.

Call a Favorite Contact

There are two ways to call a favorite contact, as outlined below.

- Add the "favorite" contact complication to your watch face, and simply tap your contact's photo or initial.

- Use the "Phone" app on your Apple Watch to browse "Favorites."

Both the Infograph and Infographic Modular watch faces support adding your "favorite contacts" as a complication. The "Favorite complication" is discussed in Chapter 4.

1. On your Apple Watch, open the Phone app.

2. Tap "Favorites."

3. Turn the Digital Crown to locate your favorite contact.

Add or Remove a Favorite Contact

1. On your iPhone, open the "Phone" app.

2. Tap "Favorites," tap the name of a contact, and swipe left to remove the contact from the favorites list.

3. Tap the plus symbol in the top left corner to add a contact.

In order for the complication to display a photo of your favorite contact, add a photo for your contact on your iPhone in the "Contacts" app.

6.17 Photos

To browse photos using the Apple Watch app "Photos," turn the Digital Crown. To add a photo library to your Apple Watch, follow the steps below.

1. Open the Apple Watch app on your iPhone.

2. Tap "My Watch," located in the left corner of the tab bar at the bottom of the screen.

3. Swipe to scroll down and tap "Photos."

4. In the section "Photo Syncing" select photo albums.

The setting "Photos Limit" controls the number of photos on your watch. Only recent photos are synced when the album size exceeds the limit. Chapter 11 includes instructions to check the number of photos on your watch.

6.18 Podcasts

Podcasts are usually original audio or video recordings. Podcasts can also be recorded broadcasts of a television or radio program, a lecture, a performance, or other events. NPR, the New York Times, MSNBC, ESPN, and iHeartRadio are a few of the Podcast providers.

The Podcast app is new with Apple Watch Series 4. Open the app on your iPhone and tap "Browse" to subscribe to a playlist. Top Charts and Featured Providers are a great starting point.

6.19 Remote Control

The Remote app is a remote control for your Apple TV or iTunes library. Once you pair your Apple Watch to your Apple TV, you tap or swipe your watch face to control the TV. Make sure your Apple Watch, iPhone and computer are all on the same Wi-Fi network.

At home, I play my iTunes music on my Yamaha amplifier that is connected to my surround sound system. After pairing the Apple Watch remote app to my iTunes computer, I can control everything from my watch.

Add Apple TV

1.   On your Apple Watch press the side button to open The Dock.

2.   Swipe and tap "Remote."

3.   Swipe up and tap "Add Device." A passcode is displayed on the screen.

4. Switch to your Apple TV and go to
    Settings -> General -> Remote.

5. Select Apple Watch and type the passcode
    displayed on your watch screen.

6. Switch to **iTunes** on your computer, and
    click on the black play icon.

7. Enter the passcode displayed on your
    watch screen.

6.20 Siri

Siri is a personal digital assistant. With
watchOS 5 Siri is now an intelligent personal
assistant. There is also a custom Siri watch
face. Siri monitors your schedule and calendar,
suggesting relevant content throughout the day.
Intelligent Siri will update you on your favorite
team's score, display one of your photos from
a year ago, or recommend a playlist for your
compute home.

Siri is also perfect for controlling your
watch. You can ask Siri to start a specific
workout, send messages, place a call, or turn on
a setting such as "Do Not Disturb."

Enable Siri on Your iPhone

1. On your iPhone, go into "Settings."

2. Scroll down and tap "Siri & Search."

In the ASK SIRI section tap the "Listen for Hey Siri" switch to toggle on or off. The switch is green when on and white when off.

Enable Siri on Your Apple Watch

1. On your Apple Watch press the Side Button.

2. Tap "Settings," and then tap General.

3. Scroll down and tap "Siri."

4. Tap the "Hey Siri" switch to toggle on or off. The switch is green when on and white when off.

Enable Raise to Speak

Raise to Speak is a new way to engage Siri. After you ask Siri a question, you can lower your wrist. Siri will gently tap your wrist when she has a response.

1. On your Apple Watch press the Side Button.

2. Tap "Settings," and then tap General.

3. Scroll down and tap "Siri."

4. Tap the "Raise to Speak" switch to toggle on or off. The switch is green when on and white when off.

Ask Siri a Question

There are two other ways to ask Siri a question.

- On your Apple Watch press and hold the Digital Crown.

- Raise your wrist and say, "Hey Siri, start my walk workout."

Siri Doesn't Respond

When Siri doesn't respond, check your internet connection. Wi-Fi and Bluetooth should both be active on your iPhone. To check connectivity on your Apple Watch, press the Digital Crown to go to your watch face. Swipe up to see Control Center and the status of connectivity.

1   On your iPhone, turn Siri off and back on.

2   On your Apple Watch open "Settings," and in the "General" section, turn Siri off and back on.

3   Turn off your Apple Watch and turn it back on. Press and hold the side button and tap "Power Off."

6.21 Stocks

The "Stocks" app can display up to 20 stocks and has four complications as shown below. Configure the list of stocks in the iPhone app.

- Current Price
- Points Change

- Percentage Change
- Market Cap

Figure 6.12   The Stock App

6.22 Stopwatch

On your Apple Watch touch the side button to open The Dock. Swipe to open the "Stopwatch" app. You can add the Stopwatch complication to your watch face as outlined in Chapter 4.

1. On your Apple Watch touch the side button.

2. Swipe to scroll and tap the "Stopwatch" app.

3. To start the Stopwatch, tap the green switch in the bottom right corner of the screen. This switch turns red to indicate the stopwatch is running.

4. To switch between analog, digital, graph, or hybrid modes, firmly press the Stopwatch screen.

Laps

The white switch in the bottom left corner of the screen is used to record laps.

1. While using the "Stopwatch" app on your watch, tap the white switch. In the analog view, the switch is in the bottom left corner of the screen.

2. The view changes and the tab bar shows "Lap" and "Start."

3. Tap "Start."

4. Tap "Lap" to record each lap. The screen displays L1, L2, etc.

5. Touch the screen and swipe up and down to see the laps.

6. Tap "Stop" when done.

7. Tap "Reset" to begin a new set of recordings.

6.23 Timer

When you open the Timer app on your watch, swipe down to see options for one minute, three minutes, 20 minutes, 30 minutes, one hour, or two hours. To set a custom timer look at the instructions below. The Timer app remembers your custom timers. Custom timers are shown in the "Recents" screen. If you like, you can add the Timer complication to your watch face as outlined in Chapter 4. For multiple timers running at the same time, a third-party app like MultiTimer comes in handy.

1. On your Apple Watch press the side button.

2. Swipe and tap to open the "Timer" app.

3. Tap "Custom."

4. Swipe to adjust hours and minutes, or turn the Digital Crown.

5. Tap "Start."

Tip: Swipe up and down within the Timer app to see options.

6.24 Walkie-Talkie

The Walkie-Talkie app is an entirely new way to communicate around the world. The Walkie-Talkie app was introduced with watchOS 5.

The Walkie-Talkie app records a voice message when you press the "Talk" button. The message is instantly sent to your friend when you release the button. A gentle tap or sound alerts you to a conversation. Connections remain open for five minutes after you stop talking. After five minutes have elapsed you must start a new conversation.

The Walkie-Talkie status icon is a stylized walkie-talkie radio. The icon appears on your watch face after you create a connection with a contact. The icon is yellow when Walkie-Talkie is turned on, and indicates your status in the Walkie-Talkie app is "available."

To use the Walkie-Talkie app check these settings.

- Apple Watch Series 1 or later with watchOS 5.

- Both watches must have connectivity through a Bluetooth connection to the iPhone, Wi-Fi, or cellular.

- Both participants must mark themselves available in the app.

- Both watches must have the Facetime app on their respective companion iPhone.

- Both participants must be logged in with a different Apple Id.

- On your Apple Watch open the Walkie-Talkie app and tap to add contacts. Swipe to set your status to available.

Invite a Friend

Before using the Walkie-Talkie app, follow these steps to connect with friends.

1. On your Apple Watch press the side button.

2. Swipe and tap to open the "Walkie-Talkie" app.

3. Tap "Add" (the plus symbol) to create a connection.

4. Swipe or turn the Digital Crown to browse through contacts. Contacts that already have Walkie-Talkie set up will appear at the top of the list in the "Suggested" section.

5. Choose a friend that has a compatible watch and tap to send an invitation.

6. After your friend accepts the invitation you can start a conversation.

Tip: Check your contact is set up with the correct Apple ID email, on your iPhone in the Contacts app.

Start a Conversation

1. On your Apple Watch press the side button.

2. Swipe and tap to open the "Walkie-Talkie" app.

3. Tap a friend.

Figure 6.13   Start a Walkie-Talkie Conversation

4. Touch and hold the "Talk" button. Release the button and your friend instantly hears what you said.

Figure 6.14   Tap to Talk

Turn the Digital Crown to control volume while using the Walkie-Talkie app.

If you turn on Silent Mode, you can still hear chimes and your friend's voice. When Theater Mode is active your Walkie-Talkie status is "unavailable." You can continue a conversation if you turn on "Do Not Disturb," but other calls are silenced.

6.25 Weather

Personally, I think the Apple weather app is awesome. Weather information is dependent on the "Location Services" configured on your iPhone. I'd encourage you to try the app, and if you're not thrilled, you could try third-party apps like Dark Sky or Carrot Weather.

Example of Weather in Motion

Let's say you have the weather complication added to your watch face. Follow these steps to view the forecast, temperature, and rainfall.

1. On your Apple Watch face, tap to select the weather complication.

2. Turn the Digital Crown to see the hourly forecast, air quality, UV index, wind speed, wind direction, and the 10-day forecast.

3. Firmly press the screen to see rain percentage, conditions, and temperature.

To remove a city, tap the city name and firmly press the display, then tap "Remove."

6.26 What's Next?

At this point, I'd like to point out the App Store showcases new third-party apps. We'll talk about a few interesting apps in the next chapter.

7. Third-party Apps

In this chapter we discuss

In April 2018 Apple began requiring that any updated app is based on watchOS 2 SDK or later. New apps had to use watchOS 4. This requirement ensured apps were native to the Apple Watch. The advantage of a native app is data is not transferred back and forth to the companion iPhone.

Apple's decision was in response to complaints about sluggish apps. Unfortunately, in response to the requirement, companies like eBay and Instagram announced their apps for Apple Watch would no longer be available. In the long run, I'm hoping Google Maps and others will rejoin the fold.

While many third-party apps work with your Apple Watch automatically, sometimes you have to create a "widget" in the iPhone app. Often smart home apps that control many custom devices use widgets. The Philips HUE lighting app and the Hunter Douglas PowerView apps currently both require you to create widgets for your smart home devices. We discuss widgets in the Smart Home section that follows.

Figure 7.1   Apple Watch HUE Widgets

Several third-party apps also provide "complications." A complication is information from an app that can be displayed on your Apple Watch Face, as discussed in Chapter 4.

Not only is it fun to search the internet for the latest "Apple Watch apps," browsing the "App

Store" for new Apple Watch apps is a great way to see what's new. On your iPhone, launch "Apple Watch" and click on "App Store." The following pages present a few interesting third-party apps. The apps are organized by category to showcase the possibilities.

7.1 Calendar and Reminders

The CARROT To-Do app is available as a stand-alone app. The To-Do app is also part of the CARROT app bundle that includes CARROT Fit, the CARROT "Artificial Superintelligence" game, CARROT Weather, CARROT Alarm, CARROT Hunger, and CARROT Sticker Pack.

For calendars, lists, and reminders take a look at these apps:

- CARROT To-Do
- Countdown Star
- Fantastical
- Things 3
- Tiny Calendar

7.2 Grocery and Cooking Apps

Consider using "To Do Lists," or timer apps that remind you to check the food cooking on your grill. These recipe, shopping, and cooking apps are also another help in the kitchen.

- CookCalc
- Cooking Time
- Grocery
- Shopper
- Vegan's Cook
- Yummly Recipes

Grocery

Grocery shopping moves to the next level with apps like "Grocery." The Grocery app complication for your watch face is perfect for grocery shopping. Tap the item as you shop to mark it complete. Firmly press the screen to "undo," "add," or switch to a different store. This app knows the route you take through the particular store and learns every time you shop.

The Grocery app uses the iOS reminders lists to store your shopping list. With a combination of iOS "Family Sharing" and an IFTTT applet that automatically links my Alexa shopping list with my iOS reminder lists, I can easily add items to my grocery list with Alexa, Google Home, or Siri. With a simple tap on our watches, everyone in our family can access our family shopping list.

Add Items to the List

Add items to your shopping list in your Mac or iCloud "Reminders." If you're like me, you could use a digital assistant to add items to your shopping list. Simply say, "Siri, add corn to my "Family reminders."

If you use another digital assistant like Alexa, you can link your iOS reminders to the Alexa shopping list with an IFTTT applet as shown below.

Enable Family Sharing

1.   On your iPhone open the Settings app and tap your name in the Apple ID banner.

2.   Swipe and tap "Setup Family Sharing." Follow the prompts to invite contacts to join your family.

Share the List with Your Family

Family sharing is active on my iPhone. My "Family" reminder list is shared with both my husband and daughter.

1. On your iPhone open the Reminders app and tap the "Family" list. Any list would work, but in this example, we're using the "Family" list.

2. Tap "Edit" and then tap "sharing." Select a contact and click add (the plus sign) to send an invitation to join the family.

Use IFTTT to link iOS and Alexa

IFTTT will automatically sync your Apple reminder list when you add an item to your Alexa shopping list. First, enable the iOS and Alexa IFTTT services and link the services to your Apple and Alexa accounts. Second, create an IFTTT applet. Note that IFTTT also has services for other digital assistants like Google Home or Microsoft Cortana.

1. In a browser login to your IFTTT account.

2. Click on "Services." Search for the service "iOS Reminders" and follow the prompts

to link your account. Repeat the steps to link your Alexa account to IFTTT.

3. Click on the button to create a **New Applet**. IFTTT stands for "If This, then That." Begin creating the applet by clicking on "This."

4. Choose the service "Alexa." Click on "Item added to your shopping list."

5. Now you want to select the trigger which is what you want to happen whenever an item is added to your Alexa shopping list. In IFTTT terms, ask yourself, when I add corn to my Alexa shopping list, do I want IFTTT to do "that?" Click on "that" and select "iOS Reminders."

6. Complete the trigger fields by selecting "Add Reminder to List." Type your iOS list name, in this case, "Family." Click Save.

7. Tap settings, the gear icon, to rename the IFTTT applet. Click save.

7.3 Entertainment

Entertainment apps encompass music apps like Shazam, apps that read books aloud like Audible, or podcast apps like Overcast. Shazam is famous for listening to a song to identify the artist and now records song titles automatically in history.

Overcast is the award-winning podcast player. Features like voice boost, smart speed, and smart playlists give you complete control. Simply install the app on your iPhone, add a podcast, select an episode to download, and you're ready to go. I love the humor the developer added under the "Add a Podcast" button, that says "Otherwise, this may not be useful." In "Settings" tap "Sync to Watch" to enable "Auto-Sync to Watch."

Not just for workouts, Amazon's Audible app reads my books out loud while I go for a walk. I was going to say when I go for a run, but I decided to be honest about my exercise level. But still, how awesome is it to go for a walk and listen to the best selling book at the same time!

- Audible
- Elevate - Brain Training
- Fandango
- iHeartRadio
- Overcast
- Shazam
- Spotify
- TuneIn

- WJXT
- Video Call Santa

In November 2018 Spotify released its first app version for Apple Watch. The app also has a complication for your watch face. Launch the app on your iPhone, and then the Apple Watch is a remote control.

7.4 Games

Normally, I'm not a big fan of digital games, but I will admit Trivia Crack can be addictive. Check out some of these games.

- Nexus Tile
- Cylinders
- Egg
- Wordie
- Komrad
- Lifeline
- Pokémon Go
- Rules
- Runeblade
- Seedling Scavenger Bingo
- Trivia Crack
- Zombies, Run!

7.5 Health and Fitness

CARROT Fit motivates you with a glimpse into your no-exercise future and focuses on 7-minute workouts. The droll verbal abuse and sly humor are unique to this app; squats are called "Territory Markers." The Apple Watch extension adds real-time heart rate data.

Similar to Apple's "Breathe" app, the "Forest-Stay Focused" app has a unique approach to being mindful. Forest is hard to describe so I'd encourage you to check it out. There's a reason it's the #1 app in 113 countries. Headspace:Meditation is another app in this category. Recent research into the neuroscience of mindfulness shows deep breathing reduces stress and has long-term health benefits.

Featured by Apple in "New Apps We Love," Gymatic uses science to identify your exercises automatically, and count your repetitions. The LoseIt! app tracks exercise and calories. The "Utility" watch face has an option to add the "LoseIt!" complication. The complication shows me how many calories remain in my daily goal.

Lifesum has won many awards with its app focused on healthy living that includes diet, exercise and healthy recipes. Do you have a loved one who forgets to eat regularly? Lifesum diligently reminds you to eat and drink water and warns when your energy level is too low. Lifesum also has complications for your watch face.

You may wonder why the following list of health apps includes Panera. In an interesting twist, when you order a meal from Panera, the calories of your meal are included in HealthKit apps. The adorable characters in Standland make it a contender for the "Stand" activity.

- Calm
- Cardiogram
- CARROT Fit
- CVS
- Daily Yoga
- Forrest
- Gymaholic
- Gymatic
- Headspace (Meditation)
- Lifesum
- LoseIt!
- Map My Run
- My Fitness Pal
- Nike Run Club
- Paddle Logger
- Panera
- Pedometer

- Runkeeper
- Runtastic
- Seven
- Standland
- Streaks
- Strava
- WorkoutDoors
- YogaGlo

Strava is a social network created specifically for athletes. You configure devices like your Peloton bike within the Strava app. The next step is to configure the Strava app with your Apple Watch. Strava also has complications for your watch face.

1. On your iPhone, launch the Strava app.

2. Create an account.

3. Follow the prompts to Connect a GPS watch or computer.

4. To make changes, click the "More" button. Tap "Settings" and then tap "Applications, Services, and Devices."

5.   Select Apple Watch. The Strava app will walk you through the settings.

6.   In "Settings under Services," tap "Health" to connect with your Apple Health app.

In Chapter 9 I touch on the topic of Sleep. Although the Health app reminds you to set a consistent time to go to sleep, at this time, it doesn't monitor your sleep patterns. To track sleep today, you need a third-party app.

The benefits of quality sleep are you are more focused and have better blood sugar regulation. And most importantly in my opinion - a fat burning growth hormone is released while you sleep!

- Auto Sleep
- Sleep ++
- Sleepio
- Sleepmatic
- Sleepwatch
- Pillow

These sleep apps read your recorded health history. Once you have established a baseline of your sleep data, you can experiment with different apps to compare their insights.

7.6 IFTTT

As an Editors' Choice app with over 17,000 reviews and a 4.7 rating, you may wonder why is the IFTTT app so special. IFTTT is an acronym for If This happens, Then do That. If you've been searching for a watch app to no avail, chances are there is already an IFTTT applet that does what you need.

Thousands of cloud services, smart home device manufacturers, and app developers have IFTTT applets. IFTTT integrates systems for delivery information, weather, pollen counts, or location (geofencing). IFTTT also controls your smart home devices like lights, thermostats, or sprinklers. With IFTTT you can also send emails, message notifications, or communicate with your digital assistant(s). Some popular IFTTT services include:

- Twitter
- Craigslist
- Amazon Cloud
- Facebook
- Logitech Harmony
- GE Appliances
- Google Drive
- eBay

- Whistle (Pet Tracker)
- Eve for Subaru

Figure 7.2   IFTTT Twitter Applet

Create IFTTT Widgets for your Apple Watch

The IFTTT iPhone app is used to configure Apple Watch widgets. These IFTTT widgets are then available on your watch.

1.   On your iPhone, open the IFTTT app.

2.   Tap the gear icon to open "Settings." Tap "Widgets," then tap "Get Widgets."

3. For example, tap "Quickly create events in Google Calendar," and then tap "Turn On."

4. When prompted, select your Google Calendar account.

5. Be sure the "Show on Apple Watch" switch is toggled on.

Create Your Own IFTTT Applets

When you visit the IFTTT web site you can search for existing applets (recipes) you can reuse, or create your own. You'll see these common services used in many of the applets.

- Location
- Date and Time
- Calendars
- Notifications

The funniest applet I've seen was entitled, "Blink the lights when the cookie jar defenses are breached." I assumed it used a motion sensor attached to the cookie jar, but in actuality it uses the "Manything" mobile app. The Manything app uses the camera on your smart phone or tablet as a surveillance device. Combined with a stand you can catch the thief (or pet) in the act!

With IFTTT you can easily create your own applets (pieces of code). When creating your applet recall that IFTTT stands for, "If This, then That."

1. Login to IFTTT and click on **New Applet**.

2. Choose a service.

3. Choose a trigger.

4. Complete the trigger fields.

5. Click on the Plus symbol to fill in "that." This is the **action**.

6. Choose an action service and save the applet.

Combine Several Actions

IFTTT has a Maker tier that allows you to combine multiple services and triggered actions. You can sign up for free at IFTTT.

1. Login to the Maker tier, or login to IFTTT and select My Applets. Click on **New Applet**. There is a choice to Build on the Platform that takes you into the Maker tier.

2. Choose a **service**.

3. Choose a **trigger**.

4. Now fill in "that" – the **action**.

5. Complete the action fields.

6. Complete remaining action fields.

7. Repeat to add more triggers and actions. Then fill in a description and save your applet.

The Applet is private (only you can use it) until you click on **Publish**.

7.7 Photography and Video

Take your mobile photography to the next level with ProCamera 8. Synonymous with action photography, it's no surprise GoPro supports the Apple Watch, and has complications for your watch face. Another app to explore is the ProCam app that captures stunning photos.

- Behance
- Camera+
- Cloud Baby Monitor
- EyeSpy

- GoPro

- Hydra

- infltr

- Moment - Pro Camera

- Opak - Photo Editor

- Photo Editor

- ProCam

- ProcCamera 8

- Video Editor

7.8 Productivity

The apps listed below are a bit varied. They include to-do lists, notes, counting, audio recording, email, calculators, financial, and others.

- Bank of America
- Budget Boss
- Calcbot
- Calc Smart
- CARROT To-Do
- Cheatsheet (Quick Notes)
- Clicker (Counts When You Tap)

- Drafts
- Facebook Messenger
- Metronome
- Mint
- Noted (Recording with Time Tags)
- Outlook
- Pcalc
- Pennies (Budget)
- Personal Capital
- Powerpoint
- Property Finder
- Recorder
- SIFT
- Slope - Finance Tracker
- Spark (email)
- Streaks
- Tempo
- Yelp

Drafts

The Drafts app is one of my favorite apps and includes a complication for your watch face. Tap the Drafts complication on your watch face, and the app opens to the "dictate" screen. Tap the microphone to dictate a recording. The screen displays the transcription text of the recording as you are dictating.

On your iPhone open the Drafts app. From the main screen, tap the paper icon in the top left corner of the screen to open the "Inbox" that lists your recordings. Tap a recording to see actions. When a recording is open in the top right corner tap the "actions" icon. Actions include mail, message, share, Google search, calendar events, List in Reminders, print and many more.

Actions are customizable and can be reordered. The first action in my app is "email me," which opens an email dialog with addresses I selected already entered.

Add a Custom Drafts Action

1. Open the Drafts app on your iPhone. In the main screen tap the actions icon in the top right corner of the screen.

2. In the actions screen top the add icon in the bottom right corner.

3. Tap the "Add New Action" button.

4. Tap the line under the "Identification" heading and enter a name for your action.

5. Swipe up and under the heading "Steps" tap the line that says "0 steps" to begin entering your steps or commands.

6. On the "Steps" screen tap the add icon in the top right corner of the screen that looks like a plus symbol. Select the "Step Type." For an email action, select a contact. You can add a subject and body text, or let the system generate it automatically from your recording.

7. In the top right corner tap "Save & Exit."

Edit or Delete an Action

1. Open the Drafts app on your iPhone. In the main screen tap the actions icon in the top right corner of the screen.

2. Tap to select an action and swipe left to right. Lift your finger, and the edit menu is shown. Tap Delete.

3. To change the order of actions tap to select an action and drag it to a new location.

7.9 Schools

Some US Universities support Student ID cards in Apple Wallet. This integration combines the "eAccounts" education app with the secure logins provided by the "Duo Mobile" authentication app.

7.10 Smart Home

Many smart home apps like the Neato robot vacuum app and the Legrand Light Control app work perfectly on the Apple Watch. Legrand encompasses smart lighting as well as electrical outlets. The Honeywell Total Connect Comfort app for thermostats also supports the Apple Watch. Hunter Douglas PowerView shades, Neato, and Legrand all work with the Alexa digital assistant. I prefer tapping my watch compared to talking to Alexa in certain situations, especially if I'm trying to be quiet. For further information on smart home technology, check out our book, "Smart Home, Digital Assistants, Home Automation and the Internet of Things."

Although I love my robotic vacuum George Jr., sometimes it's not a good time for him to vacuum. With a tap on my watch, I can direct George, Jr. to try again later. Our original Neato robot "George" didn't survive all the cat hair at our house. We're hoping George, Jr. has a long and productive life.

Figure 7.3   The Neato App

SmartThings is Samsung's solution for home automation. The SmartThings hub uses the ZigBee protocol to control lighting, security, sensors, sirens, and cameras, to name a few. In the SmartThings mobile app select "More" and then click on "My Account" to create widgets for your Apple Watch.

An unusual smart app is "Eve for Subaru." Combined with an IFTTT applet, the Subaru app controls over 400 smart home devices.

Some third-party apps require you to create a "Widget" for your Apple Watch. In the figure

225

below I am creating a widget in the Hunter Douglas app "PowerView."

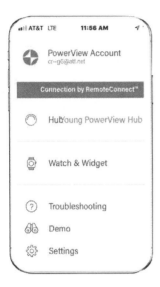

Figure 7.4   Creating a PowerView Widget

7.11 Sports and the Great Outdoors

Picture a beautiful, cool, sunny day. A gentle breeze blows as you prepare to tee off, but you're wondering just how far that green is. A glance at your Apple Watch and you are all set. The Golf Shot AR has real-time distances to the green, hazards, and over 40,000 worldwide courses. The Golf Shot integration with your

Apple Watch is like having a pro caddie on your wrist.

With Sky Guide on your Apple Watch, all you have to do is open the app and hold your watch to the sky. With the screen facing you, Sky Guide will automatically recognize the constellation patterns and orient the screen properly. Sky Guide will show you the constellations that have always been right in front of you, but you never knew existed. Sky Guide can send you a notification on your Apple Watch when an event is about to happen in the skies above your location.

There are so many apps in this category I decided to break them down into sports and outdoor. This list of sports apps is the tip of the iceberg. I'd encourage you to search the app store for sports of interest to you.

- 365Scores
- College Hoops
- Cyclemeter
- DraftKings Fantasy Sports
- ESPN
- Football Live
- Golf Shot

- Komoot
- MLB at Bat
- MyScorecard
- NFL Sunday Ticket
- Onefootball - Soccer Scores
- PitchersPal
- Slopes
- The Score

The following is a brief list of apps that you may find interesting for outdoor activities.

- AllTrails
- Big Year Birding
- GAIA
- Gardenia
- History Here
- Santa Fe Botanical
- Sky Guide
- Sunrise Sunset
- Topo Maps
- Trails
- ViewRanger

7.12 Travel

When traveling third-party apps can handle activities like directions, currency exchange, reservations, translation, and locating local events and restaurants. Check out a few of these apps to see if they would fit your lifestyle.

- App in the Air
- BMW Connected
- Citymapper
- ELK
- ETA
- Glympse
- Hilton Honors
- Hotwire
- iTranslate
- Lyft
- Magic Guide to Disney World
- Marriott
- Microsoft Translator
- New York Subway
- Poison Maps
- Toyota Vehicle Remote

App in the Air includes airport maps, live updates, reminders when to head to your gate, wait times for security, and more.

7.13 Water Sports

Paddle Logger is an interesting app for those who like to be out on the water. I'm not sure what SUP and OC are, but I do like to Kayak! Sailors will appreciate Waterspeed, an app dedicated to water sports. Real-time speed, direction, distance, heart, weather, and stats make this a popular app.

Please keep in mind Apple's guidance on water resistance and avoid scuba diving, water skiing, or high-velocity water.

- Paddle Logger
- Sail Buddy
- Waterspeed

7.14 Weather

CARROT Weather frequently rates as one of the best weather apps. You can choose between an amusing "snark" version or traditional "boring" announcer.

- CARROT Weather
- Dark Sky
- Night Sky
- Sunrise Sunset

7.15 What's Next?

Before we move on to real life (the Day to Day chapter), I would encourage you to search online for Apple Watch apps related to your interests. There are hundreds of apps now, and more added every day.

Chapter 7

8. Day to Day

In this chapter we discuss

Add Bluetooth Accessories

Charging Stands

Find Your Apple Watch

Find Your iPhone

Handoff and Continuity

Remote Control

Unlock Your Apple Watch

Unlock Your Mac

Theater and Sleep Mode

Watch Bands

What's Next?

This chapter covers those things that didn't fall into one of the previous categories. We'll also look at specific details for some common tasks.

8.1 Add Bluetooth Accessories

Low Energy Bluetooth is .3 Mbps and classic Bluetooth is up to 2.1 Mbps. When selecting hearing aids and other devices Bluetooth speed impacts direct streaming.

Workout aficionados will appreciate wireless headphones, and I have to say Apple AirPods take it to the next level. Someone, or more likely several someones, put a lot of thought into engineering AirPods. Both the Apple Watch Series 4 and AirPods are on Oprah's Favorite Things list for 2018. Airpods instantly turn on and connect to your iPhone, Apple Watch, iPad, or Mac. Double tap to activate Siri to adjust volume, make a call, or change the song. The "Elgago" Silicone strap corrals AirPods to your Apple Watch.

1. Turn on pairing mode on your Bluetooth accessory.

2. Press the Digital Crown on your Apple Watch to open the Dock.

3. Tap the gear icon to open "Settings." If you don't see the gear, touch the watch face and move your finger until you locate the gear icon.

4. Scroll and select "Bluetooth."

5. Tap to select the Bluetooth accessory.

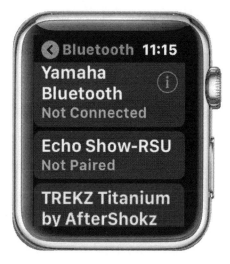

Figure 8.1   Pair Bluetooth Accessory

Hearing Aids

If you are using hearing aids look for those that are "Made for iPhone." Some models, like Phonak Audéo Marvel hearing aids, support direct Bluetooth streaming to both ears.

1. Open your hearing aid's battery doors.

2. On your iOS device, tap Settings > General > Accessibility > Hearing > MFi Hearing Devices.

3. Close the battery doors of your hearing aid. Your iOS device will search for your hearing aid.

4. Under "Devices," tap the name of your hearing aid.

5. Tap Pair when you see the pairing request on the screen. If you have two hearing aids, you will get two requests. The pairing process could take up to a minute.

Once paired the MFi Hearing Device screen has several options. By default "Control on Lock Screen" will be on. Leave it on to control your hearing aid from the Lock screen (using the Accessibility Shortcut,) or from Control Center. Chapter 10 has additional information on controlling MFi hearing aids.

Tap the audio status icon on your watch face, and turn the Digital Crown to adjust volume on your Phonak Audéo Marvel hearing aids.

8.2 Charging Stands

After paying all that money for my watch, I want a safe place to charge it. I can imagine it falling off a table onto the porcelain tile. There are lots of designs available to choose from, ranging from styles where you loop the watch on the holder, to the elegant Apple Magnetic Charging Dock where the watch rests on the tray.

Most third-party docks leverage existing charging cables. The ClearGrass Amber box also has a power bank which is ideal when traveling. It safely stores your Apple Watch and has a USB connection for charging other devices like your iPhone.

When your Apple Watch connects to the charging cable, a green lightning bolt symbol appears. The lightning bolt symbol is red when your watch needs charging. It may take a few minutes for the green lightning bolt symbol to appear if your battery level was low.

8.3 Find Your Apple Watch

Sign in to iCloud on your computer, or use the "Find my iPhone" app on your iPhone, to locate your Apple Watch. If you have an Apple

HomePod your can say, "Hey Siri, find my watch."

1. On your iPhone open the "Find My iPhone" app and sign in.

2. Tap your Apple Watch to locate your watch on a map.

3. Tap "Actions" to play a sound, erase the watch, or turn on lost mode.

8.4 Find iPhone

You may find the Control Center button "Find My iPhone" handy if you tend to misplace your iPhone as frequently as do I! Swipe up on your watch face and tap the button to instantly sound an alert on your companion iPhone. The blue button has an iPhone with signal bars. At night touch and hold the button to flash a light on your iPhone.

1. Swipe up on the Apple Watch face to open the Control Center.

2. Swipe up and tap the Find My iPhone button.

8.5 Handoff and Continuity

Handoff is part of the "Continuity" features available on Apple devices. Continuity includes Handoff, the Universal Clipboard, Auto Unlock, the Continuity Camera, SMS and MMS, Cellular Calls, and Instant Hotspot.

The Apple Watch supports Continuity for Cellular Calls, Auto Unlock, and Handoff. Handoff is a way to seamlessly switch tasks between your Apple Watch, iPad, Mac, or iPhone. Wake up your Mac while wearing your Apple Watch and Auto Unlock gives you instant access to your Mac.

The Universal Clipboard supports copying text, images, photos, or videos between Apple devices and is not included on the Apple Watch. However, you can take screenshots of the watch face and they are saved to your iPhone photos, as outlined in Chapter 3.

Handoff From Apple Watch to iPhone

When the two devices are in range, the app appears on the other device. For example, when you have mail open on your Apple Watch, on your iPhone Mail appears in the app switcher, or as an "app banner" along the bottom of your iPhone screen.

Figure 8.2   Handoff Mail

Requirements

Each device must have these settings to use the handoff feature.

- Bluetooth enabled.

- Wi-Fi enabled.

- Signed in with the same Apple ID.

• Handoff turned on.

Enable Handoff on your Mac

1. On your Mac: Choose the Apple menu, System Preferences, then click General. Select "Allow Handoff between this Mac and your iCloud devices."

2. On your iPhone, iPad, or iPod touch: Go to Settings, General, Handoff, then turn on Handoff.

Enable Handoff on your Apple Watch

1. On your iPhone open the Apple Watch app.

2. Swipe to scroll down to "Settings" and tap "General."

3. Scroll down and touch the "Enable Handoff" switch to toggle it on or off. The switch is green when on and white when off.

8.6 Remote Control

In Chapter 6 I discussed the Remote app for controlling your Apple TV or iTunes. I wanted to briefly mention these features here as a reminder of the possibilities. Make sure your Apple Watch, iPhone and computer are all on the same Wi-Fi network.

Apple TV

Once you pair your Apple Watch to your Apple TV, you tap or swipe your watch face to control the TV.

iTunes

At home, I play my iTunes music on a Yamaha amplifier connected to our whole house speakers. After pairing the Apple Watch remote app to my iTunes computer, I can control everything from my watch.

8.7 Unlock Your Apple Watch

When the auto-lock feature is enabled, you must enter a passcode to unlock your watch. You can also configure your iPhone to unlock your watch whenever you enter a passcode on your iPhone. The "Wrist Detect" feature will keep your watch unlocked as you move.

1. Open the Apple Watch app on your iPhone.

2. Tap the "My Watch" tab (bottom left).

3. Scroll down to "Passcode."

4. Scroll down and enable the setting.

8.8 Unlock Your Mac

Speaking of unlocking - did you know you can auto-unlock Mac mid-2013 or later computers with your Apple Watch? To see the version of your Mac, click on the Apple logo and then click "About this Mac." This "Continuity" feature also requires macOS Sierra or later, and that your Apple ID uses two-factor authentication. Bluetooth and Wi-Fi must be active on your Mac. Also, both devices must be signed in with the same Apple ID.

1. On your Mac from the Apple menu, select System Preferences.

2. Click "Security & Privacy," then select the General tab. Click the lock icon to allow changes.

3. Select "Allow your Apple Watch to unlock your Mac."

8.9 Theater and Sleep Mode

The first time I went to the movies my Apple Watch glowed with an alert; I was glad I had enabled the "Cover to Mute" option as I frantically covered my watch face with my palm. Right after that, I found "Theatre Mode." If I can remember to turn on Theatre Mode, I won't be that rude person that disturbs everyone around me.

1. Swipe up on the Apple Watch face to open Control Center.

2. Tap the icon for "Theatre Mode."

Silent Mode

1. Open the Apple Watch app on your iPhone.

2. Tap "My Watch," located in the left corner of the tab bar at the bottom of the screen.

3. Scroll down and tap "Sounds & Haptics."

4. Tap the "Silent mode" switch to toggle it on or off. The switch is green when on and white when off.

5. Press the side button on your Apple Watch.

6. Scroll down and tap "Settings."

7. Scroll down and tap "Sounds & Haptics."

8. Tap "Silent Mode."

8.10 Watch Bands

Changing watch bands seemed daunting to me at first, but after doing it one time I realized how simple it is.

1.   Please your watch face down on a soft surface.

2.   Press the band release button on the back on the watch and slide the band left or right to remove it from the slot.

3.   Slide the new band into the slot until you feel and hear a click.

Figure 8.3   Release Buttons for the Watch Band

The end of the watch band that slides into the slot has a top and bottom. The top has three clips. The bottom has two clips on each end with a solid piece in the middle. If you reverse the top and bottom the band will not lock in place.

8.11 What's Next?

Next up are Health and Fitness apps. I hope you agree I saved the best for last.

Chapter 8

9. Health and Fitness

In this chapter we discuss

The Apple Watch heart rate monitor and health and fitness apps work together to meet your health and fitness goals. Features like an electrical heart rate sensor, built-in electrodes, optical heart sensor, accelerometer, and gyroscope are ideal for health and fitness apps. The accelerometer can differentiate between a walk and a run and enables features like "Running Auto Pause," to identify when you're taking an exercise break.

- Activity App
- Workout App
- Breathe (Mindfulness) App
- Health App
- ECG App
- Heart Rate App

The Activity app has three goals: move, stand, and exercise. Apple calculates your exercise and stand goals for you, but does allow you to change your move goal. The goals change weekly, adapting to your lifestyle. The goals are designed to be a challenge that is within your reach.

The workout app includes walking, running, cycling, hiking, swimming, and yoga workouts, to name a few. If you don't see the workout you want, the "other" category allows you to record a workout and then give it a custom name.

The Health app displays the Activity, Workout, Mindfulness, and Heart rate records. When linked to other health apps, the Health app displays body measurements, health records, lab results, and vital statistics in one place. The Heart Rate app also shows insights into your heart rate, such as your Heart Rate Recovery results.

Finally, third-party apps link to medical devices with specific tasks like CGM, continuous glucose monitoring. The Dexcom system sensor connects to a transmitter, which communicates with a smart device. The Dexcom watch complication displays data on your Apple Watch.

9.1 Basic Settings

To ensure accurate activity logging, and accurate motion calibration and distance logging, configure these options.

- Fitness Tracking & Health
- Location Services (GPS)
- Motion, Calibration, and Distance
- Your Profile in the Health App

Motion & Fitness

1. On your iPhone, open Settings, and go to Privacy."

2. Scroll down and tap "Motion & Fitness."

3. Enable "Fitness Tracking."

4. Enable "Health."

After you enable the option for "Motion, Calibration, and Distance," Apple suggests you take a 20 minute walk outdoors away from Wi-Fi. This enables the watch to calibrate your movement with GPS location.

1. On your iPhone open "Settings" and tap "Privacy."

2. Tap "Location Services" and scroll to the bottom and tap "System Services."

3. Enable "Motion, Calibration, and Distance."

Location Services

To view your location on your watch face or in the workout app set it up on your iPhone. Location is also helpful with distance calibration.

- On your iPhone, open Settings, and go to "Privacy."

- Enable "Location Services."

- Scroll down to the list of apps, and select "Apple Watch Faces" and "Apple Watch Workout."

- Set both options to "While Using the App."

Heart Rate Alerts

Set heart rate alerts in notification settings.

- On your iPhone, open the Apple Watch app.

- Tap "Notifications."

- Tap "High Heart Rate" or "Low Heart Rate" and set the threshold.

Chapter 9

Setup the Health App

Your Apple Watch uses your personal information: height, weight, gender, and age to calculate metrics for daily activity. It also asks your activity levels. Activity levels are light, moderate, or active.

1.   On your iPhone open the Apple Watch app.

2.   Tap "My Watch," located in the left corner of the tab bar at the bottom of the screen.

3.   Scroll down to "Health."

4.   Tap "Health" and then tap "Edit."

5.   Enter your personal information and then tap "Done."

To see apps that are using your health data tap the "Sources" button in the tab bar at the bottom of the screen.

Wheelchair Mode

While "Wheelchair" mode is active the "stand goal" in the Activity app changes to a "roll goal," and the "steps" counter changes to "pushes." Two new workouts take into account different pushing conditions with varying speeds and terrain. To ensure you receive the Weekly Summary report on Monday, be sure to change the "Wheelchair" mode to "Yes" or "No." If "Wheelchair" is "Not Set," it could affect Activity Logging.

1. On your iPhone open the Apple Watch app.

2. Tap "My Watch," located in the left corner of the tab bar at the bottom of the screen.

3. Swipe up, then tap "Health."

4. Tap "Edit" in the top right corner of the screen.

5. Tap Wheelchair, and choose an option at the bottom of the screen.

9.2 The Heart Rate App

The Heart Rate app displays your current, resting, and walking average heart rate. Blood pressure monitoring, electrocardiogram monitoring, and irregular rhythm notifications were introduced with iOS 12.1.1. The optical heart sensor uses photo plethysmography (PPG) to detect your heart rate. The green LED lights paired with light-sensitive photodiodes detect the amount of blood flowing through your wrist based on green light absorption.

1. On your Apple Watch, press the Side Button.

2. Scroll and tap the "Heart Rate" app.

3. Swipe or turn the Digital Crown to see your "Resting Rate" and your "Walking Average" heart rate.

When you open the Heart Rate app on your watch it measures your heart rate every five seconds. To measure your heart rate every second, touch your finger to the Digital Crown. When you lift your finger the Heart Rate app goes back to measuring your heart rate every five seconds.

The Health app also records your Heart Rate Recovery after a workout. watchOS 4 introduced Heart Rate Recovery. Heart Rate Recovery measures your heart rate when you end a workout, and compares it to your heart rate two minutes later. So for instance, depending on your age, a heart rate recovery over 60 would be considered very good. Search the internet for the latest information on heart rate recovery and see where you stand. There is scientific evidence that suggests a low heart rate recovery indicates heart problems. Check out the "Heart Rate" app in Chapter 6 for instructions on how to view your "Heart Rate Recovery."

9.3 GymKit

Recently you may have noticed elliptical or treadmill equipment compatible with Apple's new GymKit platform. Tap your watch against the machine's NFC reader at any time during your workout. Your Apple Watch pairs with the machine, and the "Workout" app opens on your watch. Look for the green logo "Connects to Apple Watch."

For those who regularly use gym equipment, you're familiar with entering your age and weight to gauge your optimal heart rate and calculate calories burned. Until now you had two options; enter information every time you work out, or create an account and log in. The GymKit interface automatically connects with a tap of your Apple Watch, and your workout data syncs with the Health Kit app automatically. Manufacturers supporting GymKit include:

- Life Fitness (Elevation, Integrity, Discover)
- TechnoGym
- Matrix Fitness

- StarTrac

- Stairmaster

- Schwin

- Nautilus

9.4 The Activity App

The Activity app ensures you are getting enough exercise every day, and will send you reminders to stand, move, or exercise. In addition to notifications and reminders, there are special challenges, and daily coaching designed to encourage you to meet your goals. My goal is to be active enough that I'm not embarrassed to turn on "Activity Sharing Notifications" with my nieces and nephews. Activity sharing works with friends who also have an Apple Watch.

Set Activity Settings

1. Open the Apple Watch app on your iPhone.

2. Tap "My Watch," located in the left corner of the tab bar at the bottom of the screen.

3. Scroll down and tap "Activity."

4. Tap the "Stand Reminders" switch to turn off. The switch is green when on.

Share Activity with a Friend

Activity Sharing is a great way to find out just how serious your friends, or husband, are about winning. In hindsight, working out with my husband wasn't one of my better ideas. For friends who also have an Apple Watch, you can share your activity. The information listed below is shared. Personal information is not shared.

- The day's activity rings which include exercise and stand minutes.

- The number of active calories you burn throughout the day.

- Workout information including type and duration.

- Daily step counter.

Enable Sharing

You can share your activity with up to 40 friends. Use preset replies to lend encouragement, or choose a "smack talk" reply.

1. On your iPhone, open the "Activity" app.

2. In the tab bar along the bottom of your screen, tap "Sharing."

3. Tap the "add" icon in the top right corner of the screen. The icon looks like a red plus sign.

4. Tap "add" again to select a contact, or simply type the email address.

When your friend accepts your request, the next time you open the Activity app you can accept the request.

Accept a Sharing Request

Seriously, you may want to think twice before accepting an invitation from a friend (or spouse). If you want to go forward, this is how to accept the invitation.

1. On your iPhone open the Activity app.

2. Tap the "Sharing" tab.

3. Tap the account icon at the top of the screen.

4. Tap Accept or Ignore.

View Your Friend's Progress

1. On your iPhone or Apple Watch open the Activity app.

2. Tap the "Sharing" tab.

3. Tap the name of your friend to see their progress.

Enable Activity Sharing Notifications

1. Open the Apple Watch app on your iPhone.

2. Tap "My Watch," located in the left corner of the tab bar at the bottom of the screen.

3. Scroll down and tap "Activity."

4. Tap the "Activity Sharing Notifications" toggle to turn on. A green switch indicates the switch is on.

Move, Exercise, & Stand Rings

There are three rings in the Activity app: move, exercise, and stand. The idea is to close your rings every day. When the rings overlap, you've exceeded your goal. While "Wheelchair mode" is active, the "stand goal" in the Activity app changes to a "roll goal," and the "steps" counter changes to "pushes."

Move Ring

The move ring tracks steps or "pushes." Each week your Apple Watch displays a weekly summary and suggests a new weekly move goal based on your daily average for the week. Tap the plus or minus symbols, and then tap "Set Move Goal."

Figure 9.1   The Weekly Goal

Exercise Ring

Your vital statistics are used to calculate your personal exercise goal. Set vital statistics like age and sex in the Health app outlined in the next section.

Stand Ring

The stand goal is one minute every hour, for twelve hours a day.

Change Goal

Follow these steps to change your Move Goal in the app.

1. On your Apple Watch, press the Side Button.

2. Scroll and tap the Activity app.

3. Firmly press the screen and tap "Change Move Goal."

4. Use the symbols or turn the Digital Crown to adjust your goal.

5. Tap "Update."

Challenge a Friend

For a little friendly competition, challenge a friend. During a 7-day competition, you both earn points by filling your Activity rings. You can earn up to 600 points a day. When you are sharing Activity with a friend, you can reply to a notification with a "challenge." In the Activity app, you can also issue a challenge at any time.

1. On your Apple Watch, open the "Activity" app.

2. Swipe left, tap a friend, then tap "Compete."

History, Weekly Summary & Details

On Monday morning your watch displays a weekly summary, along with a new Move goal suggestion. When the weekly summary is displayed, tap the plus or minus symbols, and then tap "Set Move Goal."

Workout and Activity History

1. On your iPhone, open the "Activity" app.

2. In the bottom tap: History, Workouts, or Awards.

3. Tap a day, and then swipe up to see details.

4. Swipe to the bottom of the page to see steps, distance, and flights climbed.

Weekly Summary or Activity Details

1. On your Apple Watch open the "Activity" app. Force touch the dial (press firmly and hold) to open the options.

2. Select "Weekly Summary."

3. Scroll up to see calories, steps, distance, and flights climbed.

Activity Reminders

1. On your iPhone, select Settings and scroll to Notifications.

2. Tap "Activity," and then tap "Allow Notifications."

9.5 The Health App

The Health app stores daily logs for the Activity app. iOS 12.1.1 introduced blood pressure monitoring, Electrocardiogram monitoring, and irregular rhythm notifications. Apple's HealthKit technology includes partners like the National Cancer Institute, the National Heart Lung and Blood Institute, and Mayo Clinic. So, if you're browsing "Vitals" and wonder what normal body temperature is, you will notice a citation from Mayo Clinic. Right now, there is a beta program underway designed to store your health data in one place - the Health app of course. The list of companies supporting this feature includes LabCorp, Quest, and many hospitals and medical practices.

Your Vital Statistics

Your vital statistics are used by app algorithms to ensure your health and activity data is accurate. I'd encourage you to enter this information in the Health app. These are important settings used by fitness, exercise, health apps, and other types of apps. For example, the Fitzpatrick Skin Type Scale measures how susceptible your skin is to the sun's rays. In combination with weather apps, this information is used to predict the effects of the daily UV index.

- Birth Date
- Sex
- Blood Type
- Fitzpatrick Skin Type
- Wheelchair

Edit Your Personal Informational

1.   On your iPhone open the "Health" app.

2.   In the top right corner tap the "Account" icon that looks like a person.

3.   In the top right corner of the screen tap "Edit."

To see apps that are using your health data tap the "Sources" button in the tab bar at the bottom of the screen.

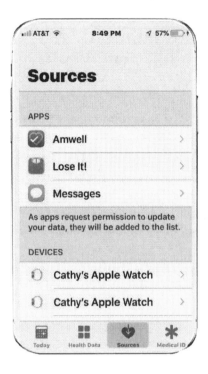

Figure 9.2   Sources for the Health App

Health Data Backups

In case you replace or upgrade your iPhone, note that if you use iCloud and your iPhone has iOS 11 and later, iCloud already has your Health and Activity data. Data is automatically kept up to date on devices where you've signed in with the same Apple ID.

The Health Data Screen

The Health Data screen has four categories: Activity, Mindfulness, Nutrition, and Sleep. Tap the Activity button to see your daily and weekly logs. The data sources are the apps you installed and linked to your Health app. For instance, my sleep app reports my sleep analysis in the "Sleep" category.

1.   On your iPhone, open the "Health" app.

2.   In the bottom tab bar tap "Health Data."

3.   In the top right corner of the screen tap "Edit."

4.   Tap Activity, Mindfulness, Nutrition or Sleep.

On the Health Data tab, you can add accounts like Quest, LabCorp, hospitals and other supported medical providers. After account linking you can see LabCorp diagnostic reports on the "Results" screen as shown below.

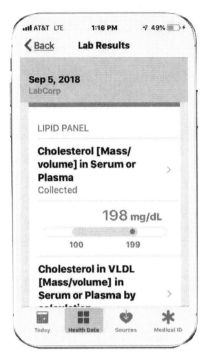

Figure 9.3   Health Data

View Heart Rate Data

The Health Data tab is also where you can view data from the "Heart Rate" app.

1.   On your iPhone, open the "Health" app.

2.   In the bottom tab bar tap "Health Data."

3. Swipe up and tap "Heart."

4. Tap the arrows at the top of the screen to move between days. Tap again to change to hour, day, week, month or year view. Tap anywhere on the graph to view the day, time, minimum and maximum information.

Explore Recommended Apps

In each Activity category, Apple includes a section called "Recommended Apps." Simply tap on the app you are interested in, and it opens in the App Store.

Although the Health app reminds you to set a consistent time to go to sleep, at this time, it doesn't monitor your sleep patterns. To track your sleep patterns, install a third-party app such as one shown below, or explore the recommended apps. Sleep affects diet, motivation, energy levels, muscle growth, and tissue repair. Proper sleep means you are more focused and have better blood sugar regulation. And most importantly in my opinion - a fat burning growth hormone is released while you sleep!

- Auto Sleep
- Sleep ++

- Sleepwatch
- Pillow

Export Health Data

Not only can you save your health data, but you can also export the data to XML files and email or message to anyone. The new ECG app has an option to "Export a PDF for Your Doctor." No more fudging our answers when your doctor asks how much you exercise a week!

As far as I know, there isn't a handy app to interpret the XML files at this time, but you can export them following these instructions.

1. On your iPhone, open the "Health" app.

2. In the top right corner tap the "Account" icon that looks like a person.

3. In the top right corner of the screen tap "Edit."

4. Scroll down and tap "Export Health Data."

9.6 The ECG App

The new ECG app arrived with watchOS 5.1.2 and iOS 12.1.1. Providing heart rate monitoring with an electrocardiogram (EKG), the app has FDA clearance in the U.S. for the ECG and atrial fibrillation detection features. The ECG app works by measuring your heart rate on your wrist while you touch the opposite hand to the Digital Crown, creating a circuit.

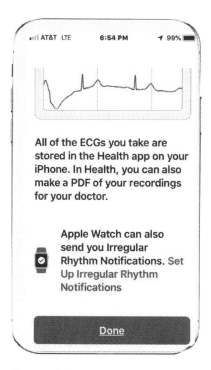

Figure 9.4   ECG App

When the latest software is installed the ECG icon appears on your watch. Follow these steps to check if you have the latest watchOS software on your iPhone.

1. Update your Apple Watch to the latest watchOS version.

2. On your iPhone, open the "Health" app. The app will prompt you to set up the ECG app.

3. Tap "Health Data," located in the tab bar at the bottom of the screen.

4. Swipe up and tap "Heart."

5. Swipe up and tap "Electrocardiogram."

Figure 9.5   Take an ECG

Export a PDF for Your Doctor

Follow these steps to take an ECG, view the ECG Detail, and then export for your doctor.

1. To take an ECG open the ECG app on your Apple Watch.

2. Touch your finger to the Digital Crown for 30 seconds.

3. On your iPhone open the "Health" app.

4. Tap "Health Data," located in the tab bar at the bottom of the screen.

5. Swipe up and tap "Heart."

6. Swipe up and tap Electrocardiogram (ECG).

7. Tap a recording, and swipe up. Tap "Export a PDF for Your Doctor."

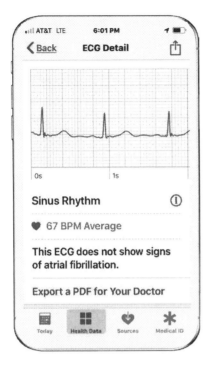

Figure 9.6   Export a PDF for Your Doctor

9.7 The Workout App

The workout app is quite sophisticated and encompasses several different components. First, we will look at the mechanics of a workout: starting a workout, viewing progress, pausing, and stopping.

Recording a workout is effortless with the Apple Watch. The watch is engineered with an accelerometer and gyroscope to correctly identify your movements, and pause workouts when you stop moving. The app even asks if you want to end the workout when it detects a change in your movements.

To help the time pass, Apple provides entertainment in the form of podcasts, music, or Audible books. Lastly, for motivation, Apple hasn't overlooked the social aspect of workouts. The watchOS 5 includes challenges and sharing your Activity data.

Running Auto Pause

Thanks to the Apple Watch accelerometer, your workout will automatically pause when you take an exercise break. Workouts automatically resume when you start moving again. Enable this feature in the Apple Watch App as shown below.

1. On your iPhone open the Apple Watch App.

2. Tap "My Watch," located in the left corner of the tab bar at the bottom of the screen.

3. Tap "Workout," then toggle "Running Auto Pause" on.

Metrics

Each workout has its own set of metrics, which you can reorder and customize to your personal preferences. Metrics vary by workout and may include the items listed below. So for example, the hiking workout uses pace, heart rate, and elevation gain.

- Duration
- Active Calories
- Heart Rate
- Average Pace
- Current Pace
- Distance
- Current Cadence
- Average Cadence
- Total Calories
- Elevation Gain
- Rolling Mile

Cadence is your steps per minute. Elevation gain ensures you will get credit when hiking those tough hills. We recently biked up a mountain in Acadia National Park, and I like knowing I get credit for that since it almost killed me. While working out, you can view metrics when you raise your wrist and turn the Digital Crown.

1. On your iPhone, open the Apple Watch app.

2. Tap "My Watch," located at the left corner of the tab bar at the bottom of the screen.

3. Tap "Workout."

4. Make sure "Workout View" is set to "Multiple Metric."

5. In the "Workouts" section tap the workout you are interested in, for example, "Outdoor Walk."

6. The top of the list displays included metrics. To remove a metric tap "Edit" in the top left corner of the screen.

7. Drag the three horizontal bars to reorder the items. Swipe left to delete.

Scroll down to the "Do Not Include" section to add metrics.

Start a Workout

1. On Your Apple Watch, press the Side Button to open The Dock.

2. Swipe and tap "Workout."

3. Swipe to find your workout, and then tap to start the workout.

Tip: When running at night - for safety try turning on the strobe flashlight. Swipe up on the Apple Watch face, tap the flashlight, and then swipe left.

Set a Goal

On your Apple Watch, select a workout as outlined above, and tap "more." The more icon looks like an ellipsis. This is also where you can set a pace alert. Goals include Calories, Distance, or Time. When you reach your goal the workout automatically ends.

Figure 9.7   Workout Options

Add to Your Workout

To add another type of workout without ending your session, open the Workout app, swipe right, then tap the "add" icon that looks like a green plus symbol.

Track Your Progress (View Metrics)

Raise your wrist and turn the Digital Crown to highlight a metric.

Listen to Music While You Workout

When working out with your Apple Watch, swipe left to play music.

Watch a Podcast or Tune in a Show

1. On our Apple Watch, open the "Podcasts" app.

2. Tap "Podcasts" in the top left corner of the screen. Tap on "iPhone" or "Library."

3. Tap Listen Now, Shows, Episodes, or Stations.

To play podcasts stored on your Apple Watch, in the Podcasts app, turn the Digital Crown to scroll and tap a podcast.

Pause Your Workout

On Your Apple Watch, press the Digital Crown and the side button at the same time. Press both buttons again to resume your workout.

End Your Workout

On Your Apple Watch, swipe right, then tap the red X.

Name Your 'Other' Workout

At the end of an "Other" workout, you can choose a name for the workout such as Barre, Core, Cross Training, Kickboxing, Dance, Badminton, Table Tennis, Tennis, Archery, AUS Football, Baseball, Basketball, Bowling, Boxing, Climbing, or Cricket. It's a long list so I'd encourage you to check it out yourself.

1. On your Apple Watch, open the "Workout" app.

2. Tap "Other."

3. Complete your workout.

4. Swipe right and tap "End."

5. Tap "Name Workout," then tap Save.

Chapter 9

Workout and Activity History

1. On your iPhone, open the "Activity" app.

2. In the bottom tap History, Workouts, or Awards.

9.8 Sample Workouts

The Apple Workout app includes these workouts: yoga, hiking, cycle, stair stepper, rower, run, walk, strength training, elliptical, or interval training. You can also expand your workouts utilizing third-party apps. These are a few features related to workouts that may be of interest.

- Listen to podcasts or Audible books. Install the apps on your Apple Watch as shown in Chapter 6.

- Set custom metrics for each workout. See the earlier section for specifics on Metrics. While working out, you can view metrics when you raise your wrist and turn the Digital Crown.

* At night turn on the strobe flashlight. Swipe up on the Apple Watch face, tap the flashlight, and then swipe left.

Running

Since I have specially fitted running shoes, I have no excuse not to run. But I don't. I find running really difficult. For those of you amazing people who have mastered the experience, there are a few ideas for your running workout.

* Listen to podcasts or Audible books. Install the apps on your Apple Watch as shown in Chapter 6.

* Enable the metrics for average and current cadence, or average and current pace. While working out, you can view metrics when you raise your wrist and turn the Digital Crown. See the earlier section for specifics on Metrics.

* At night turn on the strobe flashlight. Swipe up on the Apple Watch face, tap the flashlight, and then swipe left.

* Enable "Running Auto Pause." On your iPhone open the Apple Watch App. Tap

"Workout," then toggle "Running Auto Pause" on.

- The option "Set Pace Alert" ensures you're not running too fast or too slow. When starting an Outdoor workout tap the "More" icon (that looks like an ellipse). Then swipe up and tap "Set Pace Alert." There is an option for minutes per mile.

Swimming and Water Sports

The Workout App has an option for "Open Water Swim" or "Pool Swim" workouts. Third-party apps like Paddle Logger or "Waterspeed," are ideal for water sports. Real time speed, direction, distance, heart, weather, and stats make this a popular app.

Please keep in mind Apple's guidance on water resistance and avoid scuba diving, water skiing or high-velocity water while wearing your Apple Watch.

Turn on Water Lock

1.   On your Apple Watch, swipe up from the bottom of the screen to open Control Center.

2.   Tap the water lock icon. It looks like a drop of water.

When you're finished with your workout, turn the Digital Crown to unlock the screen and clear water from the speaker.

Yoga

There is a new Yoga Workout with Apple Watch Series 4. To avoid bumping your watch during a workout, you could change the watch orientation, or turn on water lock.

Workout Playlist

Whenever you start a workout you can automatically play music from a workout playlist you configure in your iPhone Apple watch app.

1. On your iPhone open the Apple Watch app.

2. Swipe to scroll down and tap "Workout."

3. Swipe up and tap "Workout playlist" to select a playlist for your workouts.

If you haven't already added music to your Apple Watch, checkout Chapter 6 (Watch Apps, Music), or follow these steps.

1. On your iPhone open the Apple Watch app.

2. Swipe to scroll down and tap "Music."

3. Tap the playlist or album you want to add.

9.9 Additional Workout Apps

There are third-party workout apps geared toward specific activities like sailing, kayaking, or climbing. Social networking and entertainment apps add a little fun into your workout, and apps like Forest and Breathe promote mindfulness. Check out these and other apps in Chapter 7.

• Audible

- Gymatic
- Lifesum
- Music
- Paddle Logger
- Podcasts
- Pokémon
- Runtastic
- Seedling Scavenger Bingo
- Strava

Strava is a social network created specifically for athletes. You can configure devices like your Peloton bike with Strava. The next step to complete integration is to configure the Strava app with Apple Watch.

Entertainment apps like Music, Podcasts, and Audible help your workout pass by quickly. Amazon's "Whispersync" technology allows you to listen on one device like your Apple Watch, and then seamlessly continue reading on your Kindle. How awesome is it to go for a run and listen to the new number one best seller? Honesty compels me to point out I didn't say when "I" go for a run since my exercise level is more along the lines of a brisk walk. I also want to add a shameless plug here for my books: "Smart Home, Digital Assistants, Home Automation and the Internet of Things," and as soon as Amazon accepts it this book will also be available on Audible.

Don't limit yourself to boring gym workouts. Why not do something fun for exercise? Although I don't even know what the Pokémon game is, when I read sessions can be logged as workouts and traveling certain distances for egg hatching counts as steps, I thought, "Why not?"

A few years back National Geographic had a scavenger hunt in grocery stores. I find it amazing how many countries are represented at my local grocery store. Anyway, the App Store has scavenger hunt games like Seedling Scavenger Bingo. Seedling Scavenger Bingo works on an Apple Watch or smartphone so that most everyone can play. This app would have been simply awesome for sleep over parties when my daughter was younger, or for rainy afternoons when the kids are bored and driving you out of your mind. Oops, did I just say that? Let me try the politically correct version. I loved raising my daughter, but it came with challenges.

Nature and sports enthusiasts will appreciate these apps that are available today for your Apple Watch. Several of these apps also have complications for your watch face.

- AllTrails
- Big Year Birding ABA
- Gaia GPS
- Gardenia

- Golf Shot
- Komoot
- Scavenger
- New York City Museums
- Paddle Logger
- Santa Fe Botanical
- Trails

Similar to Apple's "Breathe" app, the "Forest-Stay Focused" app has a unique approach to being mindful. Forest is hard to describe so I'd encourage you to check it out. There's a reason it's the #1 app in 113 countries.

Explore Apps

Why not search the App Store today for your favorite hobby, or try searching for sailing, hiking, nature, botany, or birding? Another option is to explore "Recommended Apps" in the Health app. Simply tap on the app you are interested in, and it opens in the App Store.

1. On your iPhone open the "Health" app.

2. In the bottom row tap "Health Data."

3. Tap Activity, Mindfulness, Nutrition, or Sleep.

4. Scroll down to the "Recommended Apps."

5. Tap the app.

9.10 What's Next?

After reviewing all the health features in this chapter, I hope you can find a place for at least some of them in your life. Now let's take a look at the accessibility features in Chapter 10.

10. Accessibility

In this chapter we discuss

In earlier chapters, we briefly mentioned haptic alerts and other accessibility features unique to the watchOS operating system. In this chapter I wanted to recap and expand on those topics. Apple has an accessibility site that showcases these features.

The work Apple has done for accessibility is outstanding. In fact, in November 2018, Apple won the prestigious Eleanor Roosevelt Humanitarian Award from the Center for Hearing and Communication for their accessibility features. The Apple Watch, watchOS, and Apple Apps work together to provide accessibility in three areas.

- Vision

- Hearing

- Physical and Motor Skills in the Workout App

In the next sections, we will discuss haptic alerts (wrist touches), accessibility settings, app integrations, wheelchair settings, and workouts.

10.1 Accessibility Shortcut

The "Accessibility Shortcut" uses the Digital Crown to turn on "Zoom" or "VoiceOver" with a triple-click.

1. Open the Apple Watch app on your iPhone.

2. Tap My Watch, and go to "General."

3. Tap Accessibility, then tap "Accessibility Shortcut."

4. Choose "VoiceOver" or "Zoom."

10.2 The Taptic Engine

The Taptic Engine encompasses "Haptic" wrist touches to alert you to an activity or message. For example, haptic alerts in the Map app gently vibrate to indicate an upcoming turn. This is a useful accessibility feature for deaf or hard of hearing drivers.

- On your iPhone open the Apple Watch app.

- In the Haptics section, tap the "Haptic Alerts" switch to toggle Haptic Alerts on or off. The switch is green when on and white when off.

To insure you receive alerts check that "Notification Center" is configured to your preferences.

Enable the Notification Indicator

1. On your iPhone, open the Apple Watch app.

2. Tap "Notifications."

3. Enable the "Notifications Indicator." When enabled a red dot at the top of your watch face indicates you have unread notifications.

10.3 Customize App Notifications

Some apps allow you to customize notification options. There is also a choice to "Mirror my iPhone," to use the same notification settings on your iPhone and Apple Watch. The choices are shown below.

- Allow Notifications
- Send to Notification Center
- Notifications Off

To set app notification options follow these steps.

- On your iPhone open the Apple Watch app.
- Tap "Notifications."
- Tap an app and select the option.

10.4 Vision

As outlined in Chapter 3, there are several settings on the "Accessibility" screen to accommodate vision. Visual enhancements include these "General" settings as well as an X-Large watch face. A complication on the X-Large watch face fills the entire screen.

- Bold Text
- Reduce Motion
- Reduce Transparency
- Side Button Click Speed
- VoiceOver
- Zoom

- On/Off Labels
- Grayscale

VoiceOver

VoiceOver is a built-in screen reader. As you move your finger over the display, each item is announced. The VoiceOver feature has 37 supported languages and works with all native apps including mail, calendar, maps, or messages.

During the initial setup process press the Digital Crown three times to activate "VoiceOver." There is also a setting to toggle the Accessibility Shortcut on as mentioned earlier.

Siri excels at toggling VoiceOver on or off. Press the Digital Crown to wake up Siri and say, "Turn on VoiceOver." Siri responds with "VoiceOver on." If you prefer you can turn on VoiceOver in "Settings."

1. On your Apple Watch, press the Side Button.

2. Tap Settings, and then tap General.

3.   Swipe to select "Accessibility."

4.   Tap "VoiceOver" to toggle on or off.

Tap twice to open an app, switch an option, or perform any action that would normally be done with a single tap. To go back to the last screen swipe a "Z" on the screen. While using VoiceOver, there is a "Screen Curtain" setting to turn off the Apple Watch display for privacy.

Set the Reading Rate

The reading rate is controlled by "Accessibility" settings.

1.   On your Apple Watch, press the Side Button.

2.   Tap "Settings," and then tap "General."

3.   Swipe to select "Accessibility."

4.   Drag the slide bar to adjust the reading rate.

Zoom

The Zoom magnification is fifteen times the native size. Turn the Digital Crown, or pinch the screen with two fingers, to control the zoom level.

On/Off Labels

The "On/Off Labels" setting will display additional label information when toggled on.

Grayscale

The "Grayscale" settings assist users where color might impair visibility. Grayscale is a system-wide setting.

10.5 Workout App

The Workout app has been optimized for wheelchair users. Two wheelchair-specific workouts take into account varying speeds, terrain, and pushing conditions. There is also a new "Time to Roll" notification. While "Wheelchair mode" is active the "stand goal" in the Activity app changes to a "roll goal," and the "steps" counter changes to "pushes."

In the Health app toggle the "Wheelchair" switch on or off. To insure you receive the Weekly Summary report on Monday, be sure to change the "Wheelchair" setting to "Yes" or

"No." If "Wheelchair" is "Not Set," it could affect Activity logging.

1. On your iPhone open the Apple Watch app.

2. Tap "My Watch" located in the left corner of the tab bar, at the bottom of the screen.

3. Swipe up, then tap "Health."

4. Tap "Edit" in the top right corner of the screen.

5. Tap Wheelchair, and choose an option at the bottom of the screen.

10.6 Hearing

If you're deaf or hard of hearing in one ear, you may miss some stereo audio or alerts. The "Mono Audio" setting plays both audio channels in both ears. You can also adjust the balance for greater volume in either ear. Toggle the "Mono Audio" switch on the "Accessibility" screen and use the slider to adjust the volume for the left or right side.

Chapter 10

1. On your Apple Watch press the Side Button.

2. Tap "Settings," and then tap "General."

3. Swipe to select "Accessibility."

4. Tap the "Mono Audio" switch to toggle the switch on or off.

5. Drag the slider bar to adjust the volume for the left or right side.

10.7 Bluetooth Accessories

Low Energy Bluetooth is .3 Mbps and Classic Bluetooth is up to 2.1 Mbps. If you are using hearing aids, look for those that are "Made for iPhone" or MFi. Some models, like Phonak Audéo Marvel hearing aids, support direct Bluetooth streaming to both ears. Chapter 8 discusses how to add Bluetooth accessories.

Hearing Aids

To support hearing aids, your Apple Watch Series 4 connects to your iPhone, and your iPhone connects to your hearing aids. Hearing Aids that support Classic Bluetooth with speeds up to 2.1 Mbps are better for direct audio streaming. For innovative hearing aid designs check out the 2019 CES Innovation Awards for accessibility products.

The MFi Hearing Device screen has several options. By default "Control on Lock Screen" will be on. Leave it on to control your hearing aid from the Lock Screen (using the Accessibility Shortcut) and from Control Center. The following is a list of MFi options.

- Play Ringtones
- Audio Routing
- Control Nearby Devices
- Audio Handoff
- Control on Lock Screen

With Audio Routing you select the default device for audio playback. Audio Handoff allows you to continue listening with your hearing aid when you switch between your iOS devices.

The "Control Nearby Devices" applies to iOS devices. Your iOS device will adjust hearing aid settings when devices are on the same Wi-Fi network and connected to your iCloud account.

1. Open your hearing aid's battery doors, or power rechargeable hearing aids off.

2. On your iPhone, tap Settings > General > Accessibility > Hearing > MFi Hearing Devices.

3. Close your hearing aid's battery doors, or turn on your rechargeable hearing aid. Your iOS device will search for your hearing aid.

4. Under Devices, tap the name of your hearing aid.

5. Tap Pair when you see the pairing request on the screen. If you have two hearing aids, you will get two requests. The pairing process can take up to a minute.

Control your MFi Hearing Aid

Control the volume of your Phonak Audéo Marvel hearing aid with your Apple Watch. Tap the audio status icon on your watch face, and turn the Digital Crown to adjust volume.

Use your iOS device to see your hearing aid's battery life, turn on Live Listen, and more. To configure your hearing aid, use "Settings" or the Accessibility Shortcut on your iPhone. Tap your hearing aid name for these options.

- View battery life.

- Unpair your hearing aid.

- Adjust volume levels for either or both hearing aids.

- "Live Listen" options (Basic, Restaurant, Outdoor, Party.)

10.8 Messaging

Text messaging is a great alternative to close captioned phone calls. Unfortunately, Facetime is not available on your watch at this time.

10.9 The Walkie-Talkie App

WatchOS 5 introduced the Walkie-Talkie app. The new Walkie-Talkie app simplifies conversations. Apple Watch Series 1 or later watches with watchOS 5 can use Walkie-Talkie. To instantly start a conversation press the side button. Release the side button to listen. Communicate with anyone who has a compatible Apple Watch. Both devices must have connectivity through a Bluetooth connection to the iPhone, Wi-Fi, or cellular. A gentle tap or sound alerts you to a conversation.

Tip: The "Tap to Talk" setting for the Walkie-Talkie app is also found under the General, Accessibility screen.

10.10 What's Next?

Just in case something goes wrong with your Apple Watch, or you have unanswered questions, the next chapter outlines basic troubleshooting steps. A few specific examples are also included.

11. Troubleshooting

In this chapter we discuss

My lazy guide to troubleshooting would be to turn your watch off and back on. A reset often fixes the problem. This chapter gathers a few of the problems I've come across in one place to save you time searching the Internet.

In the worst case scenario where I'm on my own to find the cause of the problem, I start with a few basic questions.

- Has it ever worked?

- When did the problem start?

- When was the last day I added something new?

- Is the cellular network or Wi-Fi OK?

- Did I unpair and repair the watch as outlined in Chapter 2.

- Did I force restart my watch.

- Am I running the latest version of the watchOS?

11.1 What's Wrong?

If you don't know what the problem is it can be hard to look up an answer in a particular category. This section should really be entitled, "What the heck is going on?" This topic covers those odd problems that are hard to describe.

When the screen seems locked and won't respond to anything, check if the water lock icon is displayed at the top of the screen. Turn the Digital Crown to "unlock" the screen.

When the screen display looks wonky, with impossibly large text, turn the Digital Crown to zoom out. Turn off "Zoom" on your iPhone in the Apple Watch app, as outlined in Chapter 3.

The bright white light on your screen is actually the flashlight. Press the Digital Crown to turn off the flashlight.

11.2 Apple Pay Not Working

Apple Pay is unavailable if you turned off the passcode on your Apple Watch. Follow these instructions to enable a passcode.

1. Open the Apple Watch app on your iPhone.

2. Tap "My Watch" located in the left corner of the tab bar, at the bottom of the screen.

3. Scroll down to "Passcode."

4. Touch the "Unlock with iPhone" switch to toggle the Passcode on or off.

Check the Status of the Apple Pay System

Apple maintains a system status page for all their apps. Check out https://www.apple.com/support/systemstatus/.

11.3 Battery

Several things affect battery life such as installed apps, screen colors, and connectivity. Although battery life is better on the Apple Watch Series 4 compared to previous models, the following are a few suggestions to improve battery life.

- Choose a dark watch face.

- Remove favorite apps from the Dock.

- Remove apps from your Apple Watch.

- Use Accessibility, Grayscale.

- Turn off unnecessary push notifications.

- Force quit an unresponsive App.

- Turn off "Wake Screen on Raise."

- Turn on iPhone Bluetooth.

- Use a Bluetooth chest strap for heart rate monitoring and disable the heart rate alerts.

- Turn off "Hey Siri."

Check Your Battery

Swipe up on the Apple Watch face to open Control Center, then swipe to see battery life. When in "Nightstand Mode you can tap the green lightning bolt icon to see battery life.

311

Battery Not Charging

When your Apple Watch connects to a charging cable, a green lightning bolt symbol will appear. The lightning bolt symbol is red when your watch needs charging. It may take a few minutes for the green lightning bolt symbol to appear if your battery level is low.

To troubleshoot charging try these suggestions.

1. Completely remove any plastic wrap from both sides of the charger.

2. Plug the charger into a different cable or power outlet.

3. Reset your watch.

Check Cellular Data Usage

Checking cellular data usage for apps provides a picture for how much battery power the app is using. Usage is shown for the current period, as well as for each app.

312

1. On your iPhone, open the Apple Watch app.

2. Tap the My Watch tab, then tap "Cellular."

3. Swipe to see cellular data usage for apps.

Remove Favorite Apps From the Dock

The Dock can have up to 10 favorite apps. Apps using background services over cellular networks drain your battery. Location Services, alerts, and health data syncing all drain your battery. For this reason, I remove apps I don't regularly use. In Chapter 6 I explain two methods for removing Apple Watch apps on your iPhone.

1. Open the Apple Watch app on your iPhone.

2. In the section "Installed on Apple Watch," tap the app you want to remove.

3. Ensure "Show App on Apple Watch" is not enabled. The slide bar should be white.

Turn on Grayscale

Grayscale is a system-wide setting to assist users with difficulty viewing colors. Grayscale has the added benefit of reducing battery power.

1. On your Apple Watch, press the Side Button.

2. Tap Settings, and then tap General.

3. Swipe to select "Accessibility."

4. Tap the "Grayscale" switch to toggle Grayscale on or off.

Turn Off Notifications

1. On your iPhone, open the "Apple Watch" app.

2. Tap "Notifications."

3. Tap each app and set notification options for that particular app.

Power Reserve

Your Apple Watch will automatically ask if you want to turn on Power Reserve when power drops to 10%. With Power Reserve active you can press the side button to see the current time, but you can't access any other watch features. Power Reserve mode saves power by displaying only the time. Other apps are not available when power reserve mode is active.

Turn on Power Reserve

1. Swipe up on the Apple Watch face to open "Control Center."

2. Tap the battery percentage.

3. Drag the Power Reserve slider to the right, then tap "Proceed."

Turn off Power Reserve

On the Apple Watch, press and hold the side button until you see the Apple logo. In a few seconds the logo will appear. Your watch will restart.

Turn Off Siri

1. On your Apple Watch press the Side Button.

2. Tap "Settings," and then tap General.

3. Scroll down and tap "Siri."

4. Disable "Hey Siri." The slider is green when enabled and white when disabled.

Turn Your Watch Off and Back On

1. On your Apple Watch, press and hold the side button until the menu appears.

2. Touch the "Power Off" slider and drag to the right to turn off your watch.

3. Press and hold the side button to turn your watch back on.

11.4 Calendar & Contacts

When your contacts or calendar are not synching properly try a reset.

1. On the iPhone, open the Apple Watch app.

2. Tap "My Watch," located in the left corner of the tab bar at the bottom of the screen.

3. Tap "General" and then tap "Reset."

4. Tap "Reset Sync Data."

11.5 Complications

Occasionally I've noticed that a complication won't show as available in the Apple Watch app on the iPhone. However, it is still possible to add the complication on the Apple Watch itself.

1. On your Apple Watch, press the Digital Crown to go to the Watch Face.

2. Firmly press the display and then tap "Customize."

3. Swipe to display the highlighted area to customize.

4. Turn the Digital Crown to change the highlighted feature, or select an app "Complication."

Strangely, the complication will then show in the Apple Watch app on your iPhone, but only for that particular watch face.

11.6 Can't Connect to iPhone

It doesn't happen often, but sometimes your watch won't connect to the companion iPhone. The Control Center displays connection status. A red iPhone icon with a slash indicates the connection is broken.

Figure 11.1   iPhone Connection Status Icon

On your Apple Watch face, swipe up to open Control Center. When your watch and phone are paired, a green phone icon is displayed in the top left corner of the screen as shown in Figure 11.1.

When your Apple Watch loses its connection to your iPhone, these troubleshooting steps might fix the problem.

- Disable Airplane mode on both devices.
- Restart your Apple Watch and iPhone.

11.7 Connectivity

There is no setting on your Apple Watch for Bluetooth. It is always on unless you enable Airplane Mode. If you are experiencing trouble with a Bluetooth device check the settings on that device. To fix other basic connectivity issues try these steps.

1. On your Apple Watch, swipe up on the watch face.

2. Tap to enable "Airplane mode," then tap again to disable Airplane Mode.

3. On your iPhone, go to the "Settings" and disable Bluetooth, then Re-enable it.

Am I Connected to Cellular?

The Cellular button turns green when you have a connection. The green dots show the signal strength. 4 green dots indicate the Apple Watch is connected to a cellular network.

Figure 11.2   Cellular Connection Status

Am I Connected to Wi-Fi?

The Cellular button turns white when your cellular plan is active, but your watch is connected to your iPhone or Wi-Fi.

Figure 11.3   Wi-Fi Connection Status

Global Cellular

There are two separate models for Apple Watch Series 4, optimized for the country of purchase. The LTE and UMTS bands used around the world are supported by the corresponding model.

Wi-Fi Won't Switch to Cellular

If you experience problems switching between Wi-Fi and LTE networks, these suggestions may help.

- Restart your watch.
- Install the latest watchOS.
- Check your cellular connection.

11.8 Digital Crown Not Responding

When the Digital Crown does not respond, try to isolate if it is a software or hardware issue. When the Digital Crown turns, and nothing happens, it is a software problem.

A hardware issue is when the Digital Crown will not turn. Try cleaning your watch according to Apple's instructions.

11.9 Force Restart

If your Apple Watch is not responding, you should try a force restart.

1. On your Apple Watch press and hold the Digital Crown and side button for 10 seconds.

2. Release both buttons when you see the Apple logo.

11.10 Forgotten Passcode

There are two ways to access your Apple Watch if you forget your passcode.

Unpair the Apple Watch from the corresponding iPhone. Then set up your watch again. When prompted, you can restore your watch from a backup to recover your settings.

Reset your Apple Watch and pair it once again with your iPhone.

1. Open the Apple Watch app on your iPhone.

2. Tap the "My Watch."

3. Scroll down to "General."

4. Tap "Reset."

11.11 Home Screen Views

If you are unable to switch between grid and list view on the Home screen, turn off your watch and turn it back on.

Switch Between Grid or List View

With the Home screen open, firmly press the screen and then tap either "Grid View" or "List View."

11.12 How Much Space is Available

To free up space, you could remove Apps, photos, or Music as outlined in Chapter 6.

How Much Total Space is Available

The "About" information includes these items.

- The count of songs on your watch.
- The count of photos on your watch.
- The number of applications on your watch.
- The total capacity.
- The available capacity.

1. On your iPhone open the Apple Watch app.

2. Swipe to scroll down and tap "General."

3. Tap "About" to see available capacity.

Figure 11.4   About - Capacity

11.13 Mickey Won't Announce the Time

Try these steps when Mickey or Minnie Mouse won't announce the time.

1. Check "Tap to Speak" is enabled in "Sounds & Haptics" as outlined in Chapter 2.

2. Make sure "Silent Mode" is not active in "Sounds & Haptics."

3. Turn off your Apple Watch and turn it back on. (Press and hold the side button.)

4. Try a "force restart." On your Apple Watch press and hold the Digital Crown and side button for 10 seconds. Release both buttons when you see the Apple logo.

11.14 Notifications

If you don't see notifications check your paired iPhone is connected, and the Apple Watch is not locked.

1. On your Apple Watch, press the Digital Crown to open the Home screen.

2. Swipe up from the bottom to open the Control Center.

3. In the top left corner verify the companion iPhone icon is green.

4. Ensure Wi-Fi is enabled.

5. Make sure "Do Not Disturb" is disabled.

Troubleshooting Message Notifications

There are a few things to check when you are not receiving message notifications.

1. In the Apple Watch app on your iPhone check if the setting "Mirror My iPhone" is enabled. In the Watch app open "Notifications" and then tap "Messages."

2. On your iPhone disable "Allow Notifications" and force restart your iPhone. Enable "Allow Notifications." Try turning on "Badge App Icon" and "Show on Lock Screen."

3. Check if "Mute" or "Do Not Disturb" is enabled.

4. Unlock your watch screen.

5. Force restart your watch. Press the side button and Digital Crown for three seconds until the Apple logo appears.

6. Check connectivity. Swipe up on your watch face to open the Control Panel.

7.   Check your settings for iMessage.
     iMessage allows you to send to an email
     address if that contact has an Apple
     device. On your iPhone in Settings open
     "Messages." In the section "Send &
     Receive" verify your Apple ID and SMS
     phone number.

8.   A basic test involves sending a test SMS
     message by typing in a phone number in
     the "To" section of the message.

11.15 Reset, Restore & Backups

The reset option will unpair your Apple
Watch from the corresponding iPhone. After
reset, set up your Apple Watch again as outlined
in Chapter 2, and restore from backup to recover
your settings. You can reset your Apple Watch
with the watch controls, or from your iPhone.

1.   On your Apple Watch, press and hold the
     side button until you see "Power Off."

2.   Firmly press the power off slider, and then
     release your finger.

3.   Tap "Erase all content and settings."

Turn Your Watch Off and Back On

1. On your Apple Watch, press and hold the side button until the menu appears.

2. Touch the "Power Off" slider and drag to the right to turn off your watch.

3. Press and hold the side button to turn your watch back on.

Backups & Restore

Your Apple Watch settings are automatically backed up to your iPhone. Whenever you backup your iPhone to iTunes or iCloud, your Apple Watch settings are automatically included. Backups do not include Bluetooth pairings, Apple Pay cards, or your passcode.

11.16 Screen Settings

At night you may not want the screen to light up when you move your wrist. The solution is to turn off "Wake Screen on Wrist Raise" or turn on Silent Mode.

1. On your Apple Watch press the Side Button.

2. Tap "Settings," and then tap General.

3. Scroll down and tap "Wake."

4. Scroll down to the selection "Wake Screen on Wrist Raise."

Reset Home Screen Layout to Factory Default

1. On the iPhone, open the Apple Watch app.

2. Tap "My Watch," located in the left corner of the tab bar at the bottom of the screen.

3. Tap "General" and then tap "Reset."

4. Tap "Reset Home Screen Layout."

11.17 Siri Doesn't Respond

If Siri doesn't respond with a vocal prompt check "Voice Feedback" is toggled on.

- On you iPhone, follow the steps in Chapter 9 to turn Siri off and back on.

- On your Apple Watch open "Settings" and tap "Siri." Toggle "Voice Feedback" on, and adjust the volume.

- On your Apple Watch, follow the steps to turn Siri off and back on as shown below.

- Turn off your Apple Watch and turn back on. (Press and hold the side button.)

Check your internet connection. Wi-Fi and Bluetooth should both be active on your iPhone. To check your Apple Watch, press the Digital Crown to go to your watch face. Swipe up to see Control Center and the status of connectivity.

1. On your Apple Watch press the Side Button.

2. Tap "Settings," and then tap General.

3. Scroll down and tap "Siri."

4. Touch the "Hey Siri" slider and continue holding the slider as you move it to disabled. The slider is green when enabled and white when disabled.

Check if the Siri System is Available

Apple maintains a system status page for all its apps. Check out https://www.apple.com/support/systemstatus/.

11.18 Walkie-Talkie App

To use the Walkie-Talkie app check these settings.

- Apple Watch Series 1 or later with watchOS 5.

- Both watches must have connectivity through a Bluetooth connection to the iPhone, Wi-Fi, or cellular.

- Both participants must mark themselves available in the app.

- Both watches must have the Facetime app on their respective companion iPhone.

- Both participants must be logged in with a different Apple Id.

- On your Apple Watch open the Walkie-Talkie app and tap to add contacts. Swipe to set your status to available.

The Walkie-Talkie app behaves differently when you turn on Silent Mode, Theater Mode, or Do Not Disturb. Swipe up on the watch face to open Control Center to check the status.

Silent Mode: You can still hear chimes and your friend's voice.

Theater Mode: Your Walkie-Talkie status is "unavailable."

Do Not Disturb: You can continue a conversation if you turn on "Do Not Disturb," but other calls are silenced.

11.19 Watch Not Responding

If your Apple Watch is not responding try a force restart.

1.   On your Apple Watch press and hold the Digital Crown and side button for 10 seconds.

2.   Release both buttons when you see the Apple logo.

11.20 Watch Will Not Wake

If your Apple watch won't wake when you lift your wrist, check the settings for wrist and digital crown orientation.

1. On your iPhone, open the Apple Watch App.

2. Tap the "My Watch" tab located in the bottom left corner of the screen.

3. Scroll down to "General."

4. Under "Watch Orientation" select left or right wrist.

11.21 watchOS Version

Yes, I am one of those people whose OS and app versions are usually out of date, simply because I like to control what's installed. If it works OK and there is no security issue I'm happy, and I tend to ignore update alerts. However, installing the latest version does fix some issues or security risks, so when your watch notifies you it's time to update your watchOS, follow these instructions.

1. Make sure your Apple Watch is on the charger.

2. On your iPhone open the Apple Watch app.

3. Tap "General" and then tap "Software Update."

11.22 Weekly Summary

In case you don't receive the Weekly Summary from the Activity app on Monday mornings, check your wrist orientation and wheelchair settings.

1. On your iPhone open the Apple Watch app.

2. Tap "Passcode."

3. Swipe up, then tap "Wrist Detection." A green slider bar indicates Wrist Detection is on.

4. Change the "Wheelchair" setting to "Yes" or "No."

1. On your iPhone open the Apple Watch app.

2. Tap the "My Watch" tab located in the bottom left corner of the screen.

3. Swipe up, then tap "Health."

4. Tap "Edit" in the top right corner of the screen.

5. Tap Wheelchair, and choose an option at the bottom of the screen.

Conclusion

In the course of writing this book, I discovered gaps in my knowledge and many useful features. Hopefully, you too, have found new benefits. Thank you for reading along with me through both the interesting topics, as well as the less than thrilling subjects. If the end result is you have mastered new features, it was worth it! I'd love to hear the cool things you're doing with your watch, so please don't hesitate to leave comments in a review.

Chapter 12

Notes

Notes

Chapter 12

Index

Notes

Notes

Made in the USA
Middletown, DE
20 May 2019